D1453641

EATING AND DRINKING WITH JESUS

Books by Arthur C. Cochrane
Published by The Westminster Press

*Eating and Drinking with Jesus:
An Ethical and Biblical Inquiry*

Reformed Confessions of the 16th Century (Ed.)

The Church's Confession Under Hitler

The Existentialists and God

Translator—

Otto Weber, *Karl Barth's Church Dogmatics:
An Introductory Report*

Eating and Drinking with Jesus

AN ETHICAL AND BIBLICAL INQUIRY

by ARTHUR C. COCHRANE

THE WESTMINSTER PRESS · PHILADELPHIA

Scripture quotations from the Revised Standard Version
of the Bible are copyright, 1946 and 1952, by the Divi-
sion of Christian Education of the National Council of
Churches, and are used by permission.

PUBLISHED BY THE WESTMINSTER PRESS®
PHILADELPHIA, PENNSYLVANIA

PRINTED IN THE UNITED STATES OF AMERICA

Library of Congress Cataloging in Publication Data

Cochrane, Arthur C.
    Eating and drinking with Jesus; an ethical and
biblical inquiry.

    Bibliography: p.
    1. Lord's Supper—Biblical teaching.   2. Food in
the Bible.   3. Drinking in the Bible.   I. Title.
BV823.C58   234'.163   73–22364
ISBN 0–664–20865–7

Contents

Preface

A preface affords an author an opportunity to record his gratitude to those who have assisted him directly or indirectly and to offer a sort of review of his own book. This book is an expansion and revision of the Robert Laidlaw Lectures, which I was invited to deliver at Knox Theological College, Toronto, during January and February of 1973. I am grateful to Principal Stanley Glen and to Professor David Hay for the invitation and for their warm hospitality. During the same period I was privileged to conduct a graduate seminar on the subject of the lectures at the ecumenical Toronto School of Theology. For this I am indebted to Professor Douglas Jay, the director, and to Professor Charles Hay, the director of graduate studies. The reception I was given at my alma mater, even when criticisms and disagreements were sometimes expressed, was heartwarming.

Some of the ideas presented in this book were given a sort of trial run in a seminar for ministers which I conducted during the summer of 1970 at Ghost Ranch, Abiquiu, New Mexico, a retreat center of the Board of Christian Education of The United Presbyterian Church in the U.S.A. For that rewarding experience I am indebted to its director, the Rev. Dr. James Hall. While the final draft of the manuscript was being

written in Germany during the spring of 1973, I had an opportunity to confer with various theologians and to give a lecture on the subject at the *Predigerseminar* at Hofgeismar.
Special thanks are due to Dr. Hans-Gernot Jung, director of
the Evangelical Academies in Germany, and to Dr. Christian
Zippert, Professor of Practical Theology at the seminary.
Through the good offices of Professor Helmut Gollwitzer the
lecture was published in *Junge Kirche*. It is, however, doubtful
whether the various lectures could have been given if, over a
seven-year period, a number of good students at the Dubuque
Theological Seminary and at Pittsburgh Theological Seminary
had not elected to take seminars with me on the Lord's Supper, engaging in intensive Biblical exegesis and historical studies in the church fathers and the Reformers.

The thesis that is argued in these pages has grown out of
two convictions. The first is that the so-called Sacrament of
the Lord's Supper, as it is observed in most churches, has little
relevance for modern man, precisely because it has little or
no relation to eating and drinking outside the church walls.
With the problems of poverty and hunger, and of the pro-
duction, distribution, and consumption of food, which oppress
all people in their daily lives, it has virtually nothing to do.
The Lord's Supper has no relation to people's work, their
economics, and their politics. Moreover, it has no connection
with the countless ways in which men and women eat and
drink. Through my reading of Karl Barth, and in a quite different way through my reading of Paul Tillich, I came to see
that Christendom has tended to drive a wedge—a wedge that
is foreign to the Bible—between the sacred and the secular,
the soul and the body, the spiritual and the temporal, and thus
to drive a wedge between a holy and a profane eating and
drinking. If there has ever been a separation of the "two kingdoms," between the sacred and the secular, then it is the doctrine and practice of the Lord's Supper.

In the Bible all life is lived in relation to God. There is no sphere of human activity outside of God's grace and outside of a covenant relationship with him. Whatever men do in business and commerce, at work or at play, they do or do not do to the glory of God. Israel is not first of all and in general a people which engages in all kinds of secular activities, such as sowing and reaping, buying and selling, marrying and procreating, and then in addition has a particular faith and form of worship and thus is active in a particular religious sphere in relation to God. On the contrary, everything that Israel does is done in relation to God. To be sure, this relationship is expressed in particular cultic acts. But these cultic acts are representative of the whole of life in relation to God. In the New Testament, Christians are reminded: "Whether you eat or drink, or whatever you do, do all to the glory of God."

In our day it is especially necessary that the gospel be expressed in the language of the world, that is, in relation to what modern man experiences and feels. In a day when people seem to have forgotten what it means to eat and drink, I was driven to ask about the similarity, the dissimilarity, and the connection between the Lord's Supper and eating and drinking in general. The Supper had to be seen in a wider perspective and answers had to be found to three simple, yet profound, questions: Why, what, and how may and must men and women eat and drink with Jesus? This book is an attempt to supply answers to these three questions.

As I pondered these questions I came to a second conviction related to the first, namely, that the separation between a holy and a profane eating and drinking has been due to the church doctrine that the Lord's Supper is a sacrament. By sacrament is meant a religious and cultic act whereby Jesus Christ is made present and his body and blood are eaten and drunk, whether realistically or spiritually, an act which is therefore a means of grace and a means of creating and strengthening faith. This time-honored doctrine had to go, not because supernaturalism is either incomprehensible or unacceptable to

modern man (modern man is not the measure of all things!)
but because it violates the plain teaching of Scripture and
derogates from Jesus Christ as the one means of grace, the
one Mediator of salvation and faith.

My misgivings regarding the sacrament stem from lectures
in the History of Doctrine by my revered teacher, the late
Professor Walter W. Bryden, of Knox College. These misgivings were strengthened, first by a pamphlet by Markus
Barth, *Das Abendmahl: Passamahl, Bundesmahl und Messiasmahl* (*Theologische Studien*, No. 18, 1945), then by his major
pioneering work, *Die Taufe ein Sakrament?* (1951), and
finally by the later writings of his father, Karl Barth, especially the *Church Dogmatics* IV, 4, on the doctrine of baptism. In the preface to that volume Barth acknowledged that
"in the face of the exegetical conclusions in my son's book, I
have had to abandon the 'sacramental' understanding of baptism, which I still maintained fundamentally in 1943."

In the same preface Barth explained that it was his original
plan to let Vol. IV, 4, be a chapter on Christian ethics (parallel to Vol. III, 4) as "the free and active answer of man to
the divine work and word of grace set forth in the doctrine
of reconciliation (Vol. IV, 1–3)." It was to begin with baptism, proceed to an elucidation of various practical aspects of
the Christian life in the light of the Lord's Prayer, and conclude with the Lord's Supper "as the thanksgiving which responds to the presence of Jesus Christ in His self-sacrifice and
which looks forward to His future." Due to ill health, his ad-
vancing years, and finally his death on May 10, 1968, the project was never completed. Thus he has left us with some unfin-
ished business, having suggested a fruitful line of thought to
pursue. Accordingly, in these pages an attempt is made to
present a doctrine of the Lord's Supper, and also of eating and
drinking in general, strictly from the standpoint of ethics. It
is a question of the goodness of the divine commandment to
eat and drink fulfilled in Jesus Christ and of the goodness of

human conduct in obedience to that commandment. All three questions—why, what, and how men may and must eat and drink with Jesus—are ethical questions.

The subtitle of this work is significant: *An Ethical and Biblical Inquiry*. The questions are ethical questions, but we seek to derive answers to them from "the uniquely authoritative witness" of Holy Scripture to Jesus Christ. We do so in the belief that, in spite of the literary, historical, and theological differences among the books of the Bible, the Bible is a unity, and moreover, that the Bible speaks out of the historical situation in which it was written to the situation of the church today. Let those who desire to do so debate whether our hermeneutical method is tenable! In the past the church has been preoccupied with the classical New Testament texts dealing with the so-called institution of the Lord's Supper in the Synoptic Gospels and in I Cor., ch. 11. More recently scholars have attempted to link with the Supper the feedings of the multitudes and the pre- and post-Easter meals Jesus ate with his disciples. But no one has attempted to see these and many other texts in the wider perspective of why, what, and how men may eat and drink with Jesus. I have been obliged to examine a wealth of Old and New Testament texts dealing with hunger and thirst, food and drink, eating and drinking, feasting and fasting that are seldom if ever considered in relation to the Lord's Supper.

The book is an inquiry, not only in the sense that it inquires of Scripture about the Lord's Supper and about eating and drinking in general, but as a question to the church. No individual theologian can assume to speak for the church. But it is his duty and responsibility to raise questions. He cannot claim finality or completeness, much less infallibility, for his findings. The tentative and imperfect answers presented in these pages are to be understood as questions. The church is asked whether its doctrine and practice of the Lord's Supper is not desperately in need of radical reformation, and if so, whether that reformation might not take the direction herein indicated. The question is being asked of all churches. As a theologian standing in the Reformed tradition and aware of my responsibility to and for that tradition (why else would I have published a collection entitled *Reformed Confessions of the 16th Century*?), I conceive the question to be raised in the first instance for the Reformed and Presbyterian family of churches. But I will not be surprised if other churches, especially the Roman Catholic Church, take the question more seriously. The Roman Catholic Church is in the process of reformation and renewal, whereas Protestant churches tend to imagine that they have been reformed and that no further reformation of their church services is needed.

Since the book is intended for the clergy and the laity (another un-Biblical example of the separation of the sacred and the secular!), the argument is set forth as simply and directly as possible. Technical and critical questions of exegesis, history, and theology, which are of special concern to theologians, are dealt with in the appendixes and notes at the end of the book. Even answers to the thorny and irksome questions whether Jesus is eaten in the Lord's Supper and whether the Supper is a sacrament have been relegated to the two appendixes. This has been done not only because of the complexity of the problem but also in order to indicate that it is a digression from the positive view of the Supper I have endeavored to present. It is well to "accentuate the positive"; and if we are unable to "eliminate the negative" altogether, we can at least demonstrate that it is accidental and marginal.

In conclusion I wish to record my gratitude to my brother, the Rev. Dr. Charles C. Cochrane, of Montreal, who read much of the material in its formative stage and encouraged me in my quest; to Professor Herbert Richardson, of St. Michael's College, Toronto, for his critical analysis of a preliminary draft; and to the staff of the Religious Book Department of The Westminster Press, for counsel during the preparation of the final manuscript. Above all, I wish to thank my wife, Ilsa, who, as patiently as possible, put up with a husband who even at the dinner table was often preoccupied with the problem of eating and drinking.

A. C. C.

Pittsburgh Theological Seminary

1

WHY MEN MAY
EAT AND DRINK WITH JESUS

According to the Biblical witness, men may and must eat and drink because God permits and commands them to eat and drink. The divine commandment, however, is not identical with a natural need and desire for survival in the face of death. The fulfillment of the commandment is not identical with a fierce struggle for existence. Man does not live under a cruel law of self-preservation. The creature lives from the grace of the Creator and Preserver. God's commandment frees man to eat and drink and to labor for his daily bread. Moreover, the commandment is not identical with the pleasures of taste and smell derived from eating and drinking. If men were to eat and drink simply to satisfy their appetites, they would be like those who Paul declares "do not serve our Lord Christ, but their own belly" (Rom. 16:18, marg.) and whose "god is the belly" (Phil. 3:19). Apart from God's gracious commandment there can be no truly joyful eating and drinking.

With the possible exception of Genesis there is no book in the Bible which so emphatically affirms a joyful freedom to eat and drink as Ecclesiastes. "Go, eat your bread with enjoyment, and drink your wine with a merry heart" (Eccl. 9:7), not simply because "bread is made for laughter, and wine gladdens life" (Eccl. 10:19), but because "God has already approved what you do" (Eccl. 9:7). It is a refrain that recurs throughout the book. "There is nothing better for a man than that he should eat and drink, and find enjoyment in his toil. This also, I saw, is from the hand of God; for apart from him who can eat or who can have enjoyment?" (Eccl. 2:24 f.) "It is God's gift to man that every one should eat and drink and take pleasure in all his toil." (Eccl. 3:13; cf. chs. 3:22; 5:18; 8:15.) It is incomprehensible that scholars have identified the divine permission and command to eat and drink in Ecclesiastes with Epicureanism. For the second chapter condemns all crude and refined forms of Epicureanism as vanity. The Preacher teaches that enjoyment in eating and drinking cannot be *acquired*; it can only be *received*. "It is God's gift to man" (Eccl. 3:13); it is "from the hand of God" (Eccl. 2:24–26). It cannot be *sought*; it can only be *found* (Eccl. 5:19). Apart from God's gracious authorization and justification man cannot eat and have enjoyment.[1]

The commandment rests upon God's gracious permission. He provides men with food and drink and permits them to eat and drink. The psalmist declares: "He satisfies him who is thirsty, and the hungry he fills with good things" (Ps. 107:9). It is a sign of God's steadfast love which endures forever that he "gives food to all flesh" (Ps. 136:25). Thus: "The eyes of all look to thee, and thou givest them their food in due season. Thou openest thy hand, thou satisfiest the desire of every living thing" (Ps. 145:15 f.). Extraordinary signs that God is the giver of food and drink were the provision of quail and manna in the wilderness (Ex., ch. 16) and water from the rock (Ex., ch. 17). One thinks also of Elijah drinking from the brook Cherith and being fed bread and meat morning and evening by the ravens, of how later in the midst of famine the widow of Zarephath, her household and the prophet "ate for many days" because "the jar of meal was not spent, neither did the cruse of oil fail, according to the word of the LORD" (I Kings 17:1–16).

In the New Testament the commandment to eat and drink is fulfilled in Jesus Christ. On the one hand, he is revealed as the Giver of food and drink and as the One who commands men to eat and drink. On the other hand, he is revealed as a hungry and thirsty man who eats and drinks in trust in his heavenly Father.

In the New Testament, Jesus is attested as the One apart from whom men do not eat and drink at all. He is the possibility of all eating and drinking. The works of creation and preservation have been traditionally ascribed to God the Father; the work of reconciliation, to the Son. Accordingly, it is proper to describe Jesus as the Giver of food and drink only as the Son or Word by whom and through whom the Father gives every good and perfect gift from above. In the epistles this is expressed in general theological terms as follows: Jesus is the wisdom by which God created and governs all things (I Cor. 1:30) and through whom "all things were made" and in whom "all things hold together" (Col. 1:16 f.; cf. John 1:3; Heb. 1:2 f.). In the Gospels, Jesus is depicted much more concretely as the One who supplies food and who then gives it to others. Three incidents stand out in the Gospels. First among the signs that Jesus did, according to John's Gospel, was the changing of water into wine at the wedding at Cana. Then there was the miraculous catch of fish as recorded in Luke 5:1–11, and thirdly, the feedings of the multitudes—of the five thousand (recorded by all four Gospels; Matt. 14:13–21; Mark 6:30–44; Luke 9:10–17; John 6:1–14) and of the four thousand (Matt. 15:32–39; Mark 8:1–10). These two latter themes are combined and repeated in John, ch. 21, in the accounts of the miraculous catch of fish and of the risen Jesus giving bread and fish to the disciples.

These miracles were obviously signs that Jesus is the Giver of food and drink. It is important to see, however, how Jesus provides food and drink. He is not portrayed as a wonder-worker. He goes in for no ostentatious display. At the wedding at Cana he gives three simple commands to the servants: (1) "Fill the jars with water"; (2) "Now draw some out"; and (3) "Take it to the steward of the feast." The miracle occurs with the obedience to these commonplace commands. Jesus goes in for no hocus-pocus, no incantations over the water. Indeed, we are not told that the roughly 150 gallons of water in the six huge waterpots were changed into wine. We are simply told that what was "drawn out" of the pots that had been "filled up to the brim" with water and had been taken to the chief steward had now become wine. Moreover, only the waiters who had drawn the water knew where the wine had come from. The steward did not know, and so attributed it to the bridegroom, who presumably had kept the best wine till the last. Not Jesus but the bridegroom gets the credit! If in this first of his signs Jesus manifested his glory, it was by no means a public demonstration. It was restricted to the waiters and to the disciples. Only his servants, only those who follow him and do whatever he tells them, know and confess that Jesus is the Lord of water and wine, the secret provider of food and drink at every table and at every celebration. It is given to his congregation to know and confess that he is the Giver of food and drink.

The feeding of the multitudes did not occur apart from the loaves and fish (which, in one case, were supplied by a young lad) nor apart from the distribution of the food to the crowds by the disciples. The point is made explicit in the account of the miraculous catch of fish by Jesus' command to Peter: "Put out into the deep and let down your nets for a catch" (Luke 5:4) and in the disciples' obedience: "Master, we toiled all night and took nothing! But at your word I will let down the nets." Nor were they able to land the great shoal of fish apart from the help they received from their partners in the other boat. In fact, the action of Jesus in supplying the great catch of fish was so scarcely distinguishable from the strenuous labors of the fishermen that it could easily have been attributed to "fisherman's luck." But Peter believed that the extraordinary catch was due to the blessing of Jesus that followed upon his obedience to Jesus' command. Instead of boasting of his obedience he was filled with astonishment and fear, and was convicted of his utter sinfulness: "Depart from me, for I am a sinful man, O Lord."

The proposition that Jesus is the One apart from whom men do not eat at all is in no way an excuse for idleness or carelessness. It is not an excuse for tempting God by doing nothing, on the pretext that "the Lord will provide" and is able to "command these stones to become loaves of bread" (Matt. 4:3). On the contrary, God commands men to work as a human affirmation of the life God has created and preserved (cf. I Thess. 4:11–12; II Thess. 3:6–12). It is evident that men do not eat and drink without working. But this does not mean that human work becomes the possibility of eating and drinking. For "it is in vain that you rise up early and go late to rest, eating the bread of anxious toil" (Ps. 127:2). Without the divine activity that precedes, accompanies, and follows human activity, all labor is fruitless. Human work, therefore, is in no sense a repetition, continuation, extension, or completion of God's work of providing daily bread. Man through his work does not become his own savior. Work does not make man a second God, and man's work is not divine. It is never "work for work's sake" but only work done to the glory of the Creator and Preserver of men. Nor does the commandment lay a burden upon men, as if work were a curse. On the contrary, the commandment frees man to work for his daily bread. On Jesus' lips the command, "Let down your nets," is a word of grace by which tired, disappointed, defeated, and discouraged men like Peter who "toiled all night and caught nothing" may set to work again. In spite of failures, repeated setbacks, and apparently insuperable obstacles, in spite of one's frustration and despair, yes, one's own lack of faith and hope, Christ's command overcomes all. It is the

strength to obey and to set to work with zest and joy. "But at
your word I will let down the nets." And as men do so, they
have the assurance that their labor in the Lord is not in vain
(I Cor. 15:58), for the Lord their God establishes the work
of their hands upon them (Ps. 90:17).

That Jesus is the fulfillment of the commandment to eat
and drink is attested most graphically by the feedings of the
multitudes, precisely because they occurred in a place where
there was no food and where there was no physical possibility of securing food. The crowds were in "the hills" and "in
the desert" some distance from the villages round about.[2] The
situation was comparable to that of the Children of Israel who
followed Moses into the wilderness, where they most certainly
would have perished had they not been fed with manna from
heaven.

In such an apparently hopeless situation the disciples see
nothing else but for Jesus to "send them away," even though
it was late in the day. As Jesus said, "If I send them away
hungry to their homes, they will faint on the way" (Mark
8:3; cf. ch. 6:35 f.). But Jesus gives his disciples an apparently
foolish and futile command: "You give them something to
eat" (Mark 6:37 and par.). And the astounding thing is that
in the end it is in fact the disciples who distribute the loaves
and the fish to the people! But how? In every account the agonizing questions are raised: "How can one feed these men
with bread here in the desert?" (Mark 8:4) and "Where are
we to get bread enough in the desert to feed so great a crowd?"
(Matt. 15:33). According to John's Gospel, Jesus puts the
question to Andrew: "How are we to buy bread so that these
people may eat?" The Evangelist adds: "This he said to test
him, for he himself knew what he would do" (John 6:6).
Whether the question is asked by men or whether it is put
to them by Jesus, it is always a question by which Jesus tests
men. He tests their faith, whether they believe that he knows
what he can and will do for the poor and hungry (Matt. 5:3, 6;

Luke 6:20–21) and whether they believe that he is willing and able to provide food and drink.

Philip has no answer to the question. "Two hundred denarii would not buy enough bread for each of them to get a little." (John 6:7.) But Jesus persists. He insists that the disciples are to take inventory of the food on hand. Hearing that there are five loaves and two fish, he says: "Bring them here to me" (Matt. 14:18). They are to surrender the little they have to Jesus that it may be shared among many. They are not to hoard the little they have. They are to give, not out of their abundance but out of their extreme poverty, as the churches of Macedonia later did (II Cor. 8:1–3). They are to give according to their means. In this instance their means consisted of five loaves and two fish. If there is a readiness to give willingly and cheerfully, "it is acceptable according to what a man has, not according to what he has not" (II Cor. 8:12). At any rate, the church, within which there are "not many powerful," not many rich, will always give out of its poverty, yet in the faith that "God is able to provide you with every blessing in abundance, so that you may always have enough of everything and may provide in abundance for every good work" (II Cor. 9:8).

What did Jesus actually do? Before we consider the fivefold action attributed to him, let us observe the fountain from which all his words and deeds flowed, namely, that he had "compassion on the crowd." The meaning is that Jesus suffered with sufferers. He made their passion his own and he did so in his inmost being—in his inward parts, or bowels, as the Greek word implies. Jesus is not a magician or a showman. The power by which he fed the people and still feeds the hungry is his freedom to take their hunger upon himself. Properly understood, the miracle was not a manifestation of supernatural power; it was a manifestation of genuine divine power which is perfected in weakness. It was the power of the cross. The power by which Jesus preserves life by furnishing

earthly food is the power of his death by which he becomes the
bread of life and the Savior of the world. The compassion of
Jesus is not mere sentiment: it is an act of suffering with and
for suffering mankind. Thus does he fulfill the commandment
to eat and drink. The compassion of Jesus found outward expression in five simple and commonplace actions. He (1) *took*
the bread and the fish; (2) *looked up* to heaven; (3) *blessed*
or *gave thanks*; (4) *broke*; and (5) *gave*.

Jesus *took* the five loaves and two fish. He takes the little
that men have to give. He accepts the gifts of time, talent,
energy, and money they bring him—paltry as these are. Not
because of any inherent value in them. Not as if by means of
them the problems of the world were to be solved. Not as if
there were any merit or efficacy in their gifts as such. On the
contrary, he accepts them as tokens of their gratitude, of their
faith and obedience, of their love and hope.

Jesus' actions of taking bread, looking up to heaven, and
blessing or giving thanks belong together: they describe how
Jesus said grace at meals. The use of the verb *lambanein*
("take") in the accounts of the Passover or Last Supper, in the
feedings of the multitudes, and in the meal at Emmaus is to
be explained in the same way.[3] The phrase "looked up to
heaven" simply describes the conventional Jewish attitude in
prayer.[4] In observing this custom, Jesus indicated that ulti-
mately every good and perfect gift is from the heavenly
Father, including the gift of daily food. There is no question
of Jesus' blessing the food and changing it into something
different. He rather praises the Creator, who controls the
fruits of the earth. Thus *eucharistein* ("give thanks") and
eulogein ("bless") are used interchangeably. The fact that in
Mark 8:6–7 *eucharistein* is used in connection with the loaves
and *eulogein* in connection with the fish would seem to indicate that there is no distinction of meaning. The words are
used interchangeably and are practically synonymous. It
should not be imagined that Jesus blessed the bread and thus

made possible its miraculous increase. In the New Testament, God is blessed or called blessed, as is Jesus, and blessedness is ascribed to men, but never to things.[5] Similarly "the breaking of bread," as Johannes Behm has explained, "is simply a customary and necessary part of the preparation of eating together. It initiates the sharing of the main course in every meal. Thus Jesus faithfully follows the custom as the head of the house when he breaks bread for the multitude (Mark 6:41 and par.; ch. 8:6 and par.; cf. ch. 8:19), for the disciples at the Last Supper (I Cor. 11:24; Mark 14:22 and par.), and for the two whom he joins on the way to Emmaus (Luke 24:30, 35). Cf. also Paul in Acts 20:11; 27:35; and I Cor. 10:16. It is from this breaking of bread at the commencement of the common meal in Palestinian Judaism that the common meal of the members of the primitive community in Jerusalem receives its name, Acts 2:42." [6]

Finally, Jesus *gave*. Instead of feeding himself, instead of being ministered unto, he gave of the little he had—the five loaves and the two fish! He too gave not out of his abundance but out of his poverty. In becoming poor, in giving up all that he had, he made many rich (II Cor. 8:9). No explanation for the miracle is given. Everything transpires in a perfectly normal and natural way, just as has happened at countless meals before and since. There is no reference to the power of Jesus. There is reference only to his powerlessness, to his poverty, to his giving up everything he possessed for others. His giving thanks points away from himself to his heavenly Father. Thus did the feeding of the multitude adumbrate the cross on which Jesus gave up his life for the life of the world. Thus was he manifested as the Giver of food and drink.[7]

We pause to take stock. We have been seeking an answer from Scripture to the question why men may eat and drink. We have heard the answer that God permits and commands men to eat and drink. And we have heard that the command-

ment is fulfilled in Jesus. In him the commandment or word
has become flesh. He is at once the commanding God and the
obedient man who eats and drinks in gratitude. Through him
all men are made free for a joyful eating and drinking. He—he
alone—is the answer to the question why men may and must
eat and drink. But with this insight we have not yet arrived
at the deepest reason why men may eat and drink. Eating
and drinking is not an end in itself, and the commandment is
not an end in itself. Mere existence is not an end in itself.
Men have not been created and preserved simply to subsist.
They have been created and preserved in order to live with
Jesus and to eat and drink with him. They eat and drink in
order to live in a covenant relation with God—to live from his
justifying, sanctifying, and saving grace and in obedience to all
his commandments. Man's chief end is to glorify God, and
to enjoy him forever. "For the kingdom of God does not mean
food and drink but righteousness and peace and joy in the
Holy Spirit." (Rom. 14:17.)

If according to the Biblical witness creation and covenant,
creation and reconciliation, are inseparable, we may say that
eating and drinking is an external presupposition for the history of the covenant between God and man, and that the covenant, or rather the covenant fulfilled in the reconciliation
in Jesus Christ, is the internal presupposition of all eating
and drinking. That is to say, men are commanded to eat and
drink in order to live by faith, in love, and with hope in Jesus
Christ as the One who is the justification, sanctification, and
redemption of all that sinful and mortal men do—including
their eating and drinking! They are required to take food and
drink in order to live with and for Jesus. On the other hand,
food and drink are signs, testimonies, and proclamations of
Jesus as the Bread of life and the Giver of the water of life,
and eating and drinking is a sign and a proclamation of an
eating of the bread of life and of a drinking of the water of
life. How thoughtlessly and joylessly do men eat and drink

when they do not perceive the twofold connection between covenant and preservation, and when they do not see that the commandment to eat and drink bears witness to the righteousness of God (cf. Rom. 3:21 f.)! We can make this connection clear to ourselves by a further consideration of the three instances in which Jesus was manifested as the Giver of food and drink.

When we turn our attention to the Christological and ecclesiological dimensions of the wedding at Cana, as opposed to the dimension of creation and preservation, we discover that at Cana *two* weddings were being celebrated simultaneously. There was, first, the marriage of an unnamed young couple whose supper, together with Jesus' decisive role, has already been described. Secondly, there was the celebration of the presence of the true Bridegroom with his bride, represented by his disciples. Jesus is the Bridegroom. John the Baptist is not the Christ, the Bridegroom, but the Bridegroom's "best man." For "he who has the bride is the bridegroom; the friend of the bridegroom, who stands and hears him, rejoices greatly at the bridegroom's voice." (John 3:28 f.) Jesus is the Bridegroom who keeps the new good wine of the Gospel "until now" or the wine which is "my blood of the [new] covenant, which is poured out for many for the forgiveness of sins" (Matt. 26:28). He is the Bridegroom who in everlasting faithfulness to his promise has come, not so much to establish a new marriage covenant as to fulfill, ratify, and renew the one covenant of grace God has made with man. When the Word became flesh, God, in the person of his Son, chose to bind himself to man irrevocably and indissolubly.

The incarnation of the Son of God is *the* marriage of God and man. "I . . . will be your God, and you shall be my people." (Lev. 26:12.) But in and with the election of man in Jesus Christ to be his bride, there is the special election of the one people of God to be his holy bride to bear witness to God's covenant of grace with all men. Strictly speaking, that

bride is the people of Israel; the church is now also Christ's
bride only in virtue of having been grafted into the true olive
tree and having become "fellow citizens with the saints and
members of the household of God." [8] Moreover, as the *one*
Bridegroom of the *one* people of God, Israel and the church,
Jesus commands that the jars be filled with water for the Jewish rites of purification, and changes that same water into the
wine of the "grace and truth" that came through him—in
contrast to the law which was given through Moses. Hence,
Jesus and his disciples, in contrast to the disciples of John
and the Pharisees, do not fast, but eat and drink. "Can the
wedding guests fast while the bridegroom is with them?" Indeed, they ate and drank so well that Jesus was accused of
being "a glutton and a drunkard," whereas of John, who
"came neither eating nor drinking," they said: "He has a
demon." While one may and must *distinguish* between the
two weddings, the two bridegrooms, the two brides, and between the water of purification and the wine, between Moses
and Jesus, the law and the gospel, Israel and the church, the
old covenant and the new, one must be careful not to *separate*
them, much less to oppose one to the other.

The Christological and ecclesiological dimensions of the
great catch of fish is seen in Jesus' words to Peter: "Do not be
afraid; henceforth you will be catching men." We perceive
that Jesus does not command men simply to work for their
daily bread, as if work, and eating and drinking, were ends in
themselves.[9] We now understand why Jesus had previously
said to Peter: "Put out into the deep and let down your nets
for a catch." The purpose of all work, of all eating and drinking, is for the sake of the church of Jesus Christ. All is to the
end that men may be caught for faith, love, and hope—caught
for God, to whom they belong. Human life is preserved by
work that is commanded and blessed by God in order that the
gospel may be preached and men may be called to faith and
repentance. Whether men know it or not, there is no other

justification for agriculture, manufacturing, commerce and finance, for education, science, and culture. We have not been put here merely to catch fish, but in order that men may be caught for Christ. Or put the other way round: were it not for the church, for the preaching of the good news, and for the call to faith, love, and hope, there would be no political and economic order. The world exists and mankind is preserved for the sake of the covenant that God has made with man in Jesus Christ; that is, in order that men may live with and for Jesus.

Jesus does not say: "You *should* catch men." What Peter should do is to "let down the nets." Catching men is not within Peter's power. If Peter and the church catch men, it will not be the result of their good intentions or strenuous efforts. It will be God's work just as in the miracle of the great draught of fish. Their task is not to convert unbelievers: their task is to let down the net of the gospel, which is the power of God unto salvation. It is the net which catches men for Jesus Christ, and all efforts should be concentrated upon seeing that this net and no other is lowered. Nor did Jesus say to Peter: "You *can* catch men." He who grants that success to the church, he who fulfills his own promise, is Jesus Christ, the Lord of the church. Only Jesus Christ can catch men, and he has done so since the beginning of the world and will do so until the end. Evidence that Jesus can and does catch men is the sentence at the conclusion of the passage: "And when they had brought their boats to land, they left everything and followed him."

The Christological interpretation of the feeding of the five thousand and its misunderstanding by the crowd, and even by the disciples, are recorded only in the Fourth Gospel. Since John devotes the lengthy sixth chapter to this subject, it deserves special consideration. For this chapter provides the clearest answer to our question why men are permitted and commanded to eat. The provision and the consumption of food

is a sign of the food which endures to eternal life, which the
Son of man will give (John 6:26 f.). It is a sign that Jesus is
the bread of life and that he who comes to him shall not
hunger, and he who believes in him shall never thirst (John
6:35, 41, 51).

John specifically informs his readers that "the Passover, the
feast of the Jews, was at hand" (John 6:4), evidently because
there is a connection between the feeding of the multitude,
the Passover, and Jesus. As the people of Israel were delivered
from Egypt through the sacrifice of the paschal lamb, and
then were fed with manna in the wilderness, so too Jesus, the
new Moses, the new Deliverer, feeds the hungry multitude in
the wilderness as a sign that the true paschal lamb has come
(John 1:29, 36), who is to die that he may become for them
the bread of eternal life. But the people completely misunderstand the gift of bread and fish and also the gift of manna
that their fathers had received in the wilderness. Moreover,
they completely misunderstand Jesus as their Messiah and
king and as Savior of the world. In short, the people misunderstand the divine commandment to eat and drink, precisely
because they have failed to see the ground of that commandment in the reconciling and redemptive work of God in Jesus.

What was the essence of their misunderstanding? They
were persuaded that man lives by bread alone and that the
commandment to eat entitles them "to labor for the food
which perishes" and even to use force to obtain it. Jesus had
provided them with bread and fish; ergo he is the Messiah and
Savior. So "they were about to come and take him by force
to make him king" (John 6:15). As Edwyn Hoskyns has observed, "The crowd, judging that one who is able to feed
them miraculously can also with miraculous power lead them
against the Romans, decides to appoint as king the man whom
God has manifestly appointed as His prophet." [10] Although
the miraculous feeding was a sign pointing to Jesus as the
Bread of life and the Savior of the whole world, they see him
as a political leader equipped with supernatural powers. They

see him as a political Messiah who can alleviate the world's ills. This man can deliver the nation from their Roman oppressors and win the war against poverty. As Walter Lüthi writes: "At one stroke the five thousand are welded together, so to speak, in a single will. They rise up as one man and, like the eruption of a volcano, the demand surges out, this man and no other. This man who creates bread must be our king. That almost uncanny spirit of unity which we might call mass hysteria stretches out its ghostly hand towards Jesus." The five thousand are confident that "not only five thousand, but fifty thousand or five hundred thousand: the whole nation will bear, shoulder high, this man who creates bread." [11] When it is said that the people wanted to "take him by force to make him king," the meaning is that they wanted to possess him and use him as a revolutionary leader. The word *harpazein*, variously translated "take by force," "seize," "kidnap," is a strong word. According to Matt. 11:12, violent men take the kingdom of heaven by force. They attempt to use Jesus and the gospel for their own economic and political purposes.

So "Jesus withdrew again to the hills by himself" (John 6:15). In a sense he resists the same temptations that faced him in the wilderness when he refused to change stones into bread and to fall down and worship the prince of this world and thus gain for himself "all the kingdoms of the world and the glory of them." But the people pursue him and when they find him on the other side of the sea, he says: "Truly, truly, I say to you, you seek me, not because you saw signs, but because you ate your fill of the loaves." They do not see that the food he gave them is a sign that he is the bread of life. "They seek Christ for the sake of the belly and not the signs" (Calvin). So Jesus admonishes them: "Do not labor for the food which perishes, but for the food which endures to eternal life" (John 6:27).

Jesus' meaning is not that work for one's daily bread is forbidden. On the contrary, if anyone does not work, neither will he eat (II Thess. 3:10). The purpose of eating and drink-

ing is that men may come to faith in him whom God has
sent.[12] The people rightly perceive from Jesus' words that they
are required to believe in Jesus and to believe that he is the
food that endures to eternal life. Still they demand concrete,
visible evidence and proof. "Then what sign do you do, that we
may see, and believe you? What work do you perform?" The
people are saying: Our forefathers were more fortunate. They
saw manna falling from heaven new each day. Jesus does not
deny that manna was given from heaven, but he declares that
it is not the true bread, the bread of God which comes down
from heaven and gives life to the world. "Your fathers ate the
manna in the wilderness, and they died. This is the bread
which comes down from heaven, that a man may eat of it and
not die." (John 6:49 f.) Jesus refuses to give any other sign
than himself and his word. The remainder of his discourse is
given to show how he becomes the bread of life for the world.
It is through the descent of the bread from heaven (John
6:33–47), through the sacrifice of his flesh for the life of the
world (John 6:51–58) and through his ascension (John 6:61–
62). The chapter is concluded by a passage about the Spirit
and the words of eternal life concerning the bread of life,
and about the ensuing offense and faith. Jesus Christ, in the
unity of his divinity and humanity, and in the twofold movement of the descent of the Father's Son in the form of man
into death at the hands of men and the ascent of the Son of
man to heaven whence he had come, is the *one* bread of life
for the world and therefore the *one* sacrament of creation and
salvation in which men are challenged to believe. Earthly
food is a sign of the food or bread of eternal life, and eating
and drinking are signs that men live only from the death of
God's Son.[13] According to John, the one human response to
the giving and receiving of the bread (and the water) of life
is *faith* (John 3:36; 4:39, 41; 5:24; 6:29, 35, 36, 40, 47, 64, 69).
"He who comes to me shall not hunger, and he who believes
in me shall never thirst."

Why may and must men eat? Answer: God permits and commands men to eat in order that they may come to faith and confess that Jesus is the Bread of eternal life and in order that their eating may be a sign and proclamation of his death. Thus Jesus is the justification and sanctification of all eating. Our answer, however, is still not complete. We have yet to show the profound reason why men may and must *drink*. Certainly not simply to quench their thirst. Certainly not because of the pleasure afforded by all sorts of delectable potions. And not even because man is commanded to drink! Rather, man is commanded to drink in order that he may come to drink of the water of life and may never thirst, and in order that water may be a sign of the water of life.

Jesus is the Giver of the water of life. In the New Testament the analogy between drinking earthly water and the water of life is set forth in the dialogue between Jesus and the adulterous Gentile woman of Samaria in John, ch. 4. It is introduced by the statement that Jesus, "wearied as he was with his journey" from Judea to a city of Samaria called Sychar, said to a woman who had come to draw water at Jacob's well, "Give me a drink" (John 4:3-7). Thereby is indicated that Jesus is able to give "living water" precisely *by becoming a thirsty man.* He who in himself is life and has the water of life "empties himself" and becomes a man who thirsts. Just as Jesus became the Bread of life for the world by offering up his flesh on the cross, so he becomes the Giver of the water of life, the Spirit, by taking upon himself the whole need and misery of men who thirst for water, for life, for righteousness, and for the living God. Jesus becomes the source of the water of life *for* men by suffering himself to die of thirst at the hands of men. The mystery of the church is that men receive the Holy Spirit only by becoming guilty of taking the life of Jesus. The Spirit can be poured out only after Jesus has been glorified in his death.[14]

John is the only one of the four Evangelists to record Jesus' cry, "I thirst" (John 19:28). But all four record that the soldiers (or one of them) gave him vinegar to drink. Luke says: "The soldiers also mocked him, coming up and offering him vinegar, and saying, 'If you are the King of the Jews, save yourself!'" (Luke 23:36–37). Matthew relates: "Jesus cried . . . , 'My God, my God, why hast thou forsaken me?' And some of the bystanders hearing it said, 'This man is calling Elijah.' And one of them at once ran and took a sponge, filled it with vinegar, and put it on a reed, and gave it to him to drink. But the others said, 'Wait, let us see whether Elijah will come to save him.' And Jesus cried again with a loud voice and yielded up his spirit" (Matt. 27:47–50; cf. Mark 15:34–37).

Doubtless the soldiers gave Jesus the vinegar or sour wine in order to revive him temporarily. They wanted to see, in mocking unbelief, whether Elijah would really come to take him down from the cross. Elijah did not come, no one came, and God did not intervene to save him. Moreover, instead of quenching Jesus' thirst, the vinegar only aggravated it. Thus the soldiers, as Chrysostom comments, "became more savage and increased their wrong." This time Jesus drank the cup which the Father had given him to drink (John 18:11)—drank its bitterest dregs. "When Jesus had received the vinegar, he said 'It is finished'; and he bowed his head and gave up his spirit." When he gave up "his spirit," the Spirit by which he had life, he gave it up to be the water of life for all who would believe in him.

Jesus' drinking of the bitter cup of vinegar is in marked contrast to his refusal to drink the wine which Matthew says was mingled with gall and Mark says was mingled with myrrh, and which was offered to him before the crucifixion. This was a wine drunk by royalty, and it had an intoxicating, even narcotic effect. One might imagine that the soldiers were taking pity on Jesus and were offering him a drink that would deaden his senses and ease his pain. Actually it was part of their mockery of him as a king. Some commentators think that Jesus refused the intoxicating cup because he wished to endure the utmost suffering. Certainly it was because he had resolved to drink the bitter cup of death the Father had given him and because of his vow of abstinence: "I tell you that from now on I shall not drink of the fruit of the vine until the kingdom of God comes" (Luke 22:18 and par.). Perhaps a reason for Jesus' refusal may also be found in the words which the mother of Lemuel, king of Massa, taught her son, as recorded in Prov. 31:4–7: "It is not for kings, O Lemuel, it is not for kings to drink wine, or for rulers to desire strong drink; lest they drink and forget what has been decreed, and pervert the rights of all the afflicted. Give strong drink to him who is perishing, and wine to those in bitter distress; let them drink and forget their poverty and remember their misery no more."

At any rate, in the second instance, Jesus' thirst and drinking of the cup of wrath was a fulfillment of Scripture.[15] "I looked for pity, but there was none; and for comforters, but I found none. They gave me poison for food, and for my thirst they gave me vinegar to drink." (Ps. 69:20–21.) Jesus drank the vinegar in obedience to the Father's will that he suffer the utmost of human cruelty, of man's inhumanity to man, and at the same time man's enmity to God. In his passion and death he overcame man's awful sin and death. And in suffering the extremes of hunger and thirst he bore—and bore away—the pangs of hunger and thirst of the poor and starving people of this world. Only in view of his own hunger and thirst on the cross could Jesus say: "Blessed are you that hunger now, for you shall be satisfied" (Luke 6:21). Not that starvation is a blessing! Not that the millions who die of starvation, often because of the heartlessness of the rich, are blessed because of their hunger and thirst! Not at all! Jesus ascribes blessedness to them because he knows what he will suffer for them and because he knows of the coming kingdom in which the poor will be everlastingly satisfied.

For what did Jesus thirst? Three answers may be given.

1. Jesus suffered real physical thirst. He thirsted for water
—for a cup of cool, clear water, which was denied him. To
thirst for water, however, is to thirst for life. He who has the
water of life perishes of thirst. He is able to give the water of
life for men only because he dies of thirst. That is what is
meant by the fact that, after he was already dead, "one of the
soldiers pierced his side with a spear, and at once there came
out blood and water" (John 19:33–34). This water was a sign
of the fulfillment of Jesus' words, "out of his heart shall flow
rivers of living water," that is, of the life-giving Spirit (John
7:37 ff.). Jesus is scarcely dead and the certainty of his death
established, when water streams from his body. Jesus Christ
is the source, the fountain, of the water of life *because* and
since his blood is shed. Water streams from his body only as
he sheds his blood for the life of the world.

2. Jesus thirsted not only for life but for righteousness. We
recall the beatitude: "Blessed are those who hunger and thirst
for righteousness, for they shall be satisfied" (Matt. 5:6). That
is to say: Blessed are sinners. Blessed are publicans and Pharisees. Blessed are those who have no righteousness in themselves. They are blessed only because Jesus stands in their
stead as "the one great sinner" (Barth), as the Lamb of God
who bears the sins of the world (John 1:29), as the one who,
though he knew no sin, was made sin for our sake (II Cor.
5:21), and who became "a curse for us" (Gal. 3:13). These
are blessed only because Jesus dies as *the* transgressor who can
only hunger and thirst after righteousness.

3. Jesus thirsted not only for life and righteousness but "for
God, for the living God" (Ps. 42:2). "O God, thou art my
God, I seek thee, my soul thirsts for thee; my flesh faints for
thee, as in a dry and weary land where no water is" (Ps. 63:1).
To thirst for God means to be cut off from God, to be without
God. It means to be forsaken and forgotten by God. Thus
Jesus' cry in John's Gospel, "I thirst," is equivalent to his cry

in Matthew and Mark, "My God, my God, why hast thou forsaken me?" Jesus was abandoned by God in order that we might never be forsaken; he was rejected that we might be elected in him.

As Jesus became *the* man who thirsted for the living God, and for the righteousness and life that come from God, he became the fountain of the water of life. And "whoever drinks of the water that I shall give him will never thirst" (John 4:14). "If any one thirst, let him come to me and drink. He who believes in me, as the scripture has said, 'Out of his heart shall flow rivers of living water.' " (John 7:38.) Those who would drink "living water" must come to Jesus. For Jesus is the fountain or well of living water. He "has" (John 4:11) and he "gives" it (John 4:10, 14, 15). But it is also "the gift of God" (John 4:10). This twofold giving of the water of life by God and by the Son is combined in the language of Rev. 22:1. "Then he showed me the river of the water of life, bright as crystal, flowing from the throne of God and of the Lamb"—that is, from God the Creator and Reconciler. Strictly speaking, Jesus is not the water of life but the bearer and dispenser of the water of life.[16] The water of life is God himself, not a creature of God. And water has its original and absolute reality and meaning in God; has its derivative and relative reality and meaning as earthly, created water. Moreover, the Holy Spirit is life-giving water in God before it is poured out *for us!* The Spirit is not life-giving water only in relation to men, but already in the Godhead. It is given by God the Father and the Son. Implied seems to be the *filioque* —the procession of the Spirit from the Father and the Son.— Whether this is to be understood with the Western church as a double procession or with the Eastern as a procession from the Father through the Son is a question we need not go into. Let it be sufficient to insist with both the Eastern and the Western churches that the Spirit (living water) is one with the Father and the Son and that the Son is the bearer and dispenser of the Spirit through his thirst unto death.

Jesus tells the woman of Samaria: "If you knew the gift of God, and who it is that is saying to you, 'Give me a drink,' you would have asked him, and he would have given you living water." She imagines that he is speaking about running water. She fails to see the analogy between created water and the water of life. In unconscious obedience to the divine commandment she goes each day to the well to draw water without any knowledge that it is in order that she may receive the Holy Spirit and never thirst, and in order that drinking may be a sign and proclamation of the Spirit. She taunts Jesus: "Where do you get that living water? Are you greater than our father Jacob, who gave us the well, and drank from it himself, and his sons, and his cattle?" Yet unconsciously she utters two profound truths: Jacob, with whom God renewed the covenant he had made with Abraham and Isaac, is the father of both Jews and Samaritans, and Jesus is the one greater than Jacob in that he has fulfilled the covenant and is the well of the water of life.

Jesus does not answer her mocking questions directly. He gives no sign other than that he himself is a man who needs a drink. He simply contrasts the two kinds of water and re-iterates his claim to give life-giving water. When she then says, "Sir, give me this water, that I may not thirst," Jesus, true to his promise, grants her request.

But how does Jesus give her and other men the Spirit? Neither here nor elsewhere in Scripture are we told. Mary is informed that the Holy Spirit will come upon her; Nicodemus, that "the wind blows where it wills, and you hear the sound of it, but you do not know whence it comes or whither it goes." According to Acts, the Holy Spirit is poured out on men like rain. The Greek verb *ekcheō* ordinarily refers to the pouring of liquids such as water and wine. When the Spirit is poured out, comes upon or descends upon men, it washes or cleanses them and it quenches their thirst. The first of these functions is called the baptism of the Spirit. It enters into a man or group of men and "fills them" (Luke 1:15, 41, 67; Acts 2:4; 4:8, 31; 9:17; 13:9; Eph. 5:18). In I Cor. 12:13, Paul combines both ideas: "For by one Spirit we were all baptized into one body . . . and all were made to drink of one Spirit." One thing is certain: the Spirit is given by Jesus directly and immediately. It is never mediated by any visible or audible elements. There are no channels or means by which the Spirit is conveyed. It is given quite independently of the church's ministry, though it creates that ministry. There is no sacramental drinking of the Spirit.[17]

Although the gift of the Spirit remains an inexplicable mystery of God, we do have testimonies concerning its effect. To drink the life-giving water is, according to John, ch. 4, to have one's sin and need exposed, to learn the idolatry and perversity of religions, to learn that the true worshipers shall worship the Father in spirit and in truth, to learn that salvation is from the Jews, that the hour of the coming of the Messiah has arrived, and to hear and believe Jesus when he says: "I who speak to you am he" (John 4:26). To receive the Spirit is to believe and to confess Jesus before men. The water of life welled up to eternal life not only for the woman of Samaria but for those to whom she bore witness and for those Gentiles who came to Jesus through her witness. Her leaving her water jar indicated that she had drunk the water of life and no longer thirsted for anything but to spread abroad the good news of the Messiah and Savior of the world. The result was that the people "went out of the city and were coming to him [Jesus]" (John 4:30). These people were "the fields . . . already white for harvest" whom Jesus urged his disciples to lift up their eyes to see (John 4:35). "Many Samaritans from that city believed in him because of the woman's testimony. . . . And many more believed because of his word." (John 4:39, 41.)

The Holy Spirit is the reality and possibility of the church, of men hearing, trusting, obeying, confessing, loving, and hoping in Jesus. The Spirit is the possibility of what Jesus Christ was and did, as the Bread of life *extra nos* and *pro nobis*, yes *pro mundo*, becoming an event *in nobis*, and therefore a subjective reality for certain men. It is the possibility of certain men hearing and believing the commandment to eat and drink fulfilled in Jesus, and therefore of knowing the secret meaning and purpose of all eating and drinking. The Spirit frees men for the answer given in Christ to the question why men may and must eat and drink.

Before we take leave of the commandment itself and go on to ask what and how men may eat and drink, we must understand to whom it is addressed. Is it, as it were, a religious commandment that applies only to Christians and perhaps also to Jews, whereas some other commandment, some natural law, applies to unbelievers? Are those outside the church destined to live under some utilitarian, Epicurean, or hedonistic principles? Are they at the mercy of the law of the jungle, "the survival of the fittest," of an iron law of economic determinism, or of an equally cruel law of laissez-faire, of so-called free competition, whereas Christians may live from God's gracious commandment? Are there two kingdoms, two compartments, the sacred and the secular, the spiritual and the temporal? Certainly not! God's gracious commandment applies to all men and all men live under it—in obedience or disobedience —whether they have heard, believe, and know it or not. However, through the gift of the Holy Spirit the church is given to hear and believe the divine commandment to eat and drink as attested in the Scriptures of the Old and New Testaments. It is given the freedom to eat and drink in obedience to the commandment. It has been given to know the secret of all eating and drinking and it has been given the task of proclaiming that secret from the housetops to all peoples. The eating and drinking of the congregation, that is, what the New Testament calls the "Lord's Supper" or "breaking of bread," is to be exemplary for all eating and drinking. When the congregation, assembled in the name of Jesus and therefore in the power of his self-revelation, partakes of a common meal, it does so in a conscious and deliberate remembrance of Jesus and in order to proclaim his death. It is to be a demonstration of why, what, and how all men may eat and drink. We are now ready for our second question: *What* may and must men eat and drink?

2

WHAT MEN MAY
EAT AND DRINK WITH JESUS

The general answer that Paul gave to the question *what* men may eat and drink is: "Everything created by God is good, and nothing is to be rejected if it is received with thanksgiving" (I Tim. 4:4). This rule is valid not only for the Christian congregation but for all men. It is clear, not only from the meals that Jesus ate with his disciples before and after his resurrection but also from the "breaking of bread" in Acts, ch. 2, and the "Lord's Supper" in I Cor., ch. 11, that the early church partook of a meal that consisted of all sorts of meat, fish, bread, vegetables, fruits, and drink. The Lord's Supper did not consist of a crumb of bread and a sip of wine; it was a meal. The simplest yet most necessary reform of the Lord's Supper in our congregations is that it must become again a meal for the nourishment of the physical body. In these pages we will give many reasons why it should be a meal. But a primary and obvious reason is that the Lord's Supper is to be a sign that men are free to eat and drink all things and that they are to do so in remembrance of Jesus who is the Giver of food and drink for the sustenance of our bodies. A meal provided by the Lord is a sign of the grace of creation and preservation.

But, it may be asked, was not the Lord's Supper itself restricted to bread and wine? Certainly not! In the accounts of the Last Supper (or Passover) in the Synoptics and in I Cor., ch. 11, we are told that Jesus took bread and wine that were part and parcel of a meal. He commanded that they be eaten and drunk as signs of his body, which was given for us, and of the new covenant in his blood. Because of the special significance attached to bread and wine in Scripture, bread and wine should be served every time the congregation eats and drinks together—but *only as integral parts of a meal!* There should be bread and wine in abundance, so that everyone may have as much as he needs. This does not mean that other foods may not be provided, such as meat, fish, fowl, vegetables, and fruit, or that other drinks may not be provided, such as water, milk, tea, coffee, beer, and soft drinks. For reasons of health or conscience some may not be able to drink wine. Moreover, in some parts of the world wine and bread may not be available. We must not be legalistic or moralistic at this point. But ordinarily, because of Scriptural and traditional associations, bread and wine should be part of the meal for the nourishment of the body, and not just for purely symbolic purposes.[1]

Usually the main course at the Lord's Table, but also at every meal, will consist of meat, fowl, or fish. Now it is by no means obvious that the congregation and all men may eat meat. It was not the case at the beginning of creation and it will not be so at the end with the consummation of all things. In the creation stories in the first two chapters of Genesis we read: "And God said, 'Behold, I have given you every plant yielding seed which is upon the face of all the earth, and every tree with seed in its fruit; you shall have them for food. And to every beast of the earth, and to every bird of the air, and to everything that creeps on the earth, everything that has the breath of life, I have given every green plant for food.' And it was so" (Gen. 1:29–30; cf. ch. 2:9a, 16). In Isa. 11: 6–9 we read: "The wolf shall dwell with the lamb, and the leopard shall lie down with the kid, and the calf and the lion and the fatling together, and a little child shall lead them. The cow and the bear shall feed; their young shall lie down together; and *the lion shall eat straw like the ox*. The sucking child shall play over the hole of the asp, and the weaned child shall put his hand on the adder's den. They shall not hurt or destroy in all my holy mountain; for the earth shall be full of the knowledge of the LORD as the waters cover the sea" (cf. Hos. 2:18; Isa. 65:25). The diet prescribed in these passages is vegetarian. Not until after the Fall and the Flood do we read: "Every moving thing that lives shall be food for you; and as I gave you the green plants, I give you everything" (Gen. 9:3). The time of natural history, that is, the time between the creation and consummation of all things, is the time when the peace between God and man, between man and his fellowman, and also among animals, has been shattered. It is the time when there is a fierce struggle for existence involving the slaughter of animals, and alas! the killing of men, women, and children in military and economic warfare. But it was not so at creation and it will not be so at the consummation. The time between the beginning and the end is the time when man may be carnivorous.

In the light of the goodwill of the Creator and Redeemer of all things, on what possible ground is it permitted to men to eat the flesh of birds, fish, and animals? We can do no better than to repeat Karl Barth's answer:

> The slaying of animals is really possible only as an appeal to God's reconciling grace, as its representation and proclamation. It undoubtedly means making use of the offering of an alien and innocent victim and claiming its life for ours. Man must have good reasons for seriously making such a claim. His real and supposed needs certainly do not justify it. He must be authorised to do so by his acknowledgement of the faithfulness and goodness of God. . . . Man sins if he does it without this authorisation. He sins if he presumes to do it on his own author-

ity. He is already on his way to homicide if he sins in the killing of animals, if he murders an animal. He must not murder
an animal. He can only kill it, knowing that it does not belong
to him but to God, and that in killing it he surrenders it to
God in order to receive it back from Him as something he
needs and desires. The killing of animals in obedience is possible only as a deeply reverential act of repentance, gratitude
and praise on the part of the forgiven sinner in face of the One
who is the Creator and Lord of man and beast. The killing of
animals, when performed with the permission of God and by
His command, is a priestly act of eschatological character. It
can be accomplished with a good conscience only as we glance
backward to creation and forward to the consummation as the
boundaries of the sphere in which alone there can be any question of its necessity. It can be achieved only in recollection of
the reconciliation of man by the Man who intercedes for him
and for all creation, and in whom God has accomplished the
reconciliation of the world with Himself.[2]

Barth's interpretation of the commandment to eat meat in
Gen. 9:3 is borne out by the forms and meanings of sacrifices
in the Old Testament. Julius Wellhausen, Hans-Joachim
Kraus, Roland de Vaux, H. H. Rowley, and other Old Testament scholars have shown that the flesh of animals was not
intended first for eating but as a sacrifice to God. It belonged
to him, and then it could be eaten.[3] Now that Jesus Christ
has become *the* Lamb of God who takes away the sins of the
world, now that the animal sacrifices in the Old Testament
have been fulfilled in his death, now that they are seen to be
signs and figures of his flesh, which has been offered up once
and for all for the life of the world, all eating of meat is permitted and commanded as a sign of our sin and guilt, of our
inhumanity, and of our forgiveness and reconciliation for
Christ's sake, and as a sign that we live solely from his death.
"A meal which includes meat is a sacrificial meal. It signifies
a participation in the reconciling effect of the animal sacrifice
commanded and accepted by God as a sign. It presupposes,

therefore, that God demands and will accept the surrender of the life of the animal for that of man as a substitutionary sign, and man's participation in the reconciliation thereby signified" [4]—namely, reconciliation through the death of God's own Son as a lamb that is slain.

If this explanation is correct, then all carnivorous eating is a sign and a proclamation of the death of Jesus and of the truth that we live only from his death. However, it will be in the Lord's Supper, eaten by the congregation in the name of Jesus, that this truth will be known and declared. It is our conviction that in the liturgy of the Supper, or at any rate in the sermon, the congregation should be instructed in the tremendous significance of meat-eating. It is a sign that the peace between God and man and between man and man, which has been shattered through man's sin and fall, has been restored in Jesus Christ and will be directly manifested at his final parousia. It will also be a sign for the congregation and for all men that man is required to be kind to animals.[5]

In view of the distinction between clean and unclean animals which is prescribed in Lev., ch. 11, and Deut. 14:3–21 and which was abolished in Acts, chs. 10, 11, and 15, it is also by no means something that may be taken for granted when Christians and all men may now eat pork. The distinction between clean and unclean animals was a provisional cultic sign of the special election and calling of Israel among all peoples, a sign of the special covenant God made with his people (Lev. 11:44 f.; 20:25–26; Deut. 14:2). It was a sign of the holiness and separateness of Israel among the nations, a sign that involved the very existence of this people, and therefore a sign pointing to the holiness and otherness of God among all the gods of the heathen. Of course, the special election of Israel had nothing to do with nationalistic pride and was not based on any merit on the part of Israel over against other nations (Deut. 7:7–8). Although Israel was to be God's "own possession among all peoples," this did not mean that the other nations did not belong to God. "For all the earth is mine." Israel was to be "a kingdom of priests and a holy nation" (Ex. 19:5–6), "a light for revelation to the Gentiles" (Luke 2:32).

Why precisely certain animals, birds, etc., were declared to be clean and others unclean is uncertain. Gerhard von Rad has suggested that certain animals were disqualified by the cult of Yahweh because they had been used by certain cults as sacrifices to divine powers.[6] But this would scarcely account for all the animals, birds, reptiles, and insects disqualified. Nor can the list be divided along hygienic lines. It is true that the meats which the law permitted are wholesome, but then so are some of the forbidden animals and seafood. To be sure, Gentile peoples have by natural instinct abhorred the eating of some of the animals forbidden in the law—but not all! It will be best, therefore, to abide by the fact that the distinction between clean and unclean animals is one which God has "set apart for you to hold unclean" because he has "separated you from the peoples." [7]

That Christians and all men may now eat all kinds of meat, fowl, and seafood is grounded upon the fact that what God has cleansed in Jesus Christ is no longer common or unclean. Through his blood Christ has broken down the dividing wall between Jews and Gentiles and has made possible a table fellowship among them and also among all races and nations. He is the ground of Christian fellowship in which all racial, national, and social barriers are broken down. Christ is our peace, Christ is our unity, in eating and drinking as well as in all human intercourse. Precisely because the blood of Christ cleanses us from all unrighteousness, we who are Gentiles need to confess the judgment of Israel's law upon us, namely, that in ourselves we are unclean. The congregation should be instructed, and it should acknowledge that the predatory and scavenger animals, birds, and reptiles listed in Lev., ch. 11, and Deut., ch. 14, are so many types of our impurity. We need not indulge in allegorical speculations concerning the ways in which the clean and unclean living beings are figures of Jews and Gentiles. Let it be enough for us to confess with the Canaanite or Syrophoenician woman that we are the dogs who eat the crumbs from their master's table (Matt. 15:27; Mark 7:28). As we eat pork at the Lord's Table or in our homes, let it be a reminder to us of our impurity and of God's superabundant grace whereby we have been admitted to the covenant which God has made with Israel and which he has never abrogated (Eph., ch. 2; Rom., chs. 9 to 11; I Peter 2: 9–10). It is by grace, the grace of our Lord Jesus Christ, that we have been grafted into the olive tree and, as a sign thereof, may now eat all things.[8] Therefore, when Paul declared, "Nothing is to be rejected if it is received with thanksgiving" (I Tim. 4:4), he did not mean a thanksgiving for food but a thanksgiving for Christ, in and through whom we may eat all things.

As God's commandment permits his creatures to eat all things, so they are free to drink all things. "Therefore let no one pass judgment on you in questions of food and drink." (Col. 2:16.) The general rule holds: "Nothing is unclean in itself" (Rom. 14:14). "There is nothing outside a man which by going into him can defile him" (Mark 7:15; cf. Matt. 15: 11). Chief among the drinks commanded in Scripture are water, milk, and wine (Deut. 14:26; Prov. 31:6 f.). Wine is commanded "to gladden the heart of man" (Ps. 104:15; cf. Eccl. 9:7; 10:19) and as good for one's stomach and ailments (I Tim. 5:23). Jesus and his disciples drank wine, and he was accused of being a drunkard. He provided wine for the wedding feast at Cana. There is, therefore, no warrant in Scripture for prohibiting the use of wine or beer at the Lord's Supper, or for restricting the beverage to grape juice, as is done in many denominations in English-speaking countries. Nor is there any warrant in Scripture for total abstinence from alcoholic beverages or for prohibition laws such as were passed in the United States and Canada following World War I and later repealed.

However, alcoholism has been such an acute problem in the countries of the Christian West where the liberty of the Christian is proclaimed (in contrast to Islam) that it must be recognized that gluttony and drunkenness are consistently condemned throughout the Old and New Testaments. Moderation and temperance are inculcated. In the New Testament churches gluttony and drunkenness constituted an abuse of the Lord's Supper. Paul rebuked the Corinthians because "in eating, each one goes ahead with his own meal, and one is hungry and another is drunk" (I Cor. 11:21). The same abuses are condemned in Jude 12 and II Peter 2:13. Jude 12 reads: "These are blemishes [or reefs] on your love feasts, as they boldly carouse together." II Peter 2:13 reads: "They are blots and blemishes, reveling in their love-feasts (*agapais*)," though other well-attested authorities have *apatais* ("deceptions" or "lusts"). The RSV follows the latter reading, and renders it "dissipations." [9] It is more than likely that Paul had the Lord's Supper in mind when he condemned excesses in eating and drinking as "the works of darkness" and admonished Christians to conduct themselves "becomingly as in the day, not in reveling and drunkenness, not in debauchery and licentiousness, not in quarreling and jealousy. But put on the Lord Jesus Christ, and make no provision for the flesh, to gratify its desires" (Rom. 13:12–14; cf. Gal. 5:19–21; I Cor. 6:9–11). Although Paul is lenient toward "the immoral of this world" and does not judge outsiders—presumably because they have not yet come to know the Lord Jesus Christ—he insists that the Christian congregation may not associate with anyone who bears the name of brother if he is guilty of immorality, idolatry, and drunkenness. The congregation is "not even to eat with such a one." One guilty of such immorality is to be judged and excommunicated (I Cor. 5:9–13). For temperance and sobriety are among the marks that distinguish the Christian fellowship from the world. "Let the time that is past suffice for doing what the Gentiles like to do, living in licentiousness, passions, drunkenness, revels, carousing, and lawless idolatry. They are surprised that you do not now join them in the same wild profligacy, and they abuse you." (I Peter 4:3 f.) If one is filled with the Spirit by which one sings and gives thanks in the name of the Lord Jesus Christ, one must not "get drunk with wine, for that is debauchery" (Eph. 5:18–20).

It is evident that in the Lord's Supper the church is to set a good example of how men and women may celebrate without going to excess. But this does not mean that the Supper is to be limited to a morsel of bread and a sip of wine, much less that the drink is to be limited to nonalcoholic grape juice. Moderation, temperance, self-control, and self-restraint are required at the Lord's Table and in all eating and drinking.[10]

Nevertheless, we are bound to ask whether there are special circumstances in which certain individuals might be required to abstain from alcoholic beverages. According to Lev. 10:8–11, the priests were forbidden to drink wine or strong drink when they entered into the tent of meeting. The reason for this temporary prohibition was that they were charged with distinguishing "between the holy and the common, and between the unclean and the clean" and with teaching "the people of Israel all the statutes which the Lord has spoken to them by Moses." Since "the lips of a priest should guard knowledge, and men should seek instruction from his mouth, for he is the messenger of the Lord of hosts" (Mal. 2:7; cf. Ezek. 44:21), it is especially incumbent upon teachers, preachers, and theologians that they abstain from alcoholic beverages while they are engaged in the study, interpretation, and proclamation of God's law. One might argue that this injunction has been abolished with the abolition of the Old Testament priesthood were it not for the fact that in the New Testament bishops and elders are particularly required to be temperate and not addicted to wine (I Tim. 3:2 f.; Titus 1:7). "God especially limited his priests in this respect, lest the vigor of their minds, and rectitude, and integrity of judgment, should be impaired by drinking" (Calvin).

Total abstinence in the Bible is confined to two groups—the Nazirites and the Rechabites.[11] They represented something like ascetic orders which, by their exclusive devotion to Yahweh, were an encouragement to Israel to remain faithful to Yahweh in the face of temptations to compromise with the pagan worship and customs of the Canaanites among whom they lived. Thus, Amos attests that God had "raised up some of your sons for prophets and some of your young men for Nazirites" and condemns the Israelites because they had "made the Nazirites drink wine and commanded the prophets, saying, 'You shall not prophesy'" (Amos 2:11 f.).[12] Gerhard von Rad has observed that Acts 21:23 ff. reports the last trace of the custom of the Nazirites. This raises the question whether the Nazirites and Rechabites have any relevance for us under the gospel. Certainly the precise regulations prescribed for them are no longer binding upon Christians. Nevertheless, they remind us that the commandment to eat and drink all things is not a timeless and universal principle; it includes the freedom to abstain from wine and strong drink.

It cannot be overlooked that in the New Testament churches there were those who did not eat flesh or drink wine (Rom. 14:1 f.), who did not marry (I Cor. 7:25 f.), and who held no possessions (Matt. 10:9 f.; Acts 2:44 f.).[13] Christian individuals and groups may therefore have the freedom to take voluntary vows of poverty, chastity, and abstinence in order to be free of anxiety "about worldly affairs" and to render a special witness over against the world and a worldly church. In all ages of the church there have been ascetic and monastic movements. These movements have often been rightly accused of escapism, quietism, otherworldliness, legalism, moralism, and works-righteousness. No doubt in many instances these and other criticisms were valid. No doubt the protest of the Reformers against monasticism in the sixteenth century was justified. But abuses do not invalidate the freedom to renounce the things of this world when the intention is to attend more diligently to works of charity, to preaching and teaching, and to pastoral and social work. In a day when society seems to be preoccupied with money, sex, success, alcohol, and drugs, even those who enjoy an evangelical freedom may be grateful for the witness of those who have taken voluntary vows of abstinence, celibacy, chastity, poverty, and anonymity.

The presence of such groups in the congregations of the New Testament led to conflicts between the "strong" and the "weak"—between those who were free to eat and drink all things and those who were vegetarians and total abstainers. Although these two styles of Christian life embraced all eating and drinking, it seems evident (especially from I Cor. 10: 19–21) that the conflict must have come to a head as the congregation ate the Lord's Supper in their meetings together. In the church at Rome there were "disputes over opinions" (Rom. 14:1). The two parties were despising and passing judgment upon one another (Rom. 14:3, 4, 10, 13). They were putting "a stumbling block or hindrance [offense] in the way of a brother" (Rom. 14:13). This led to excluding, or not "welcoming" one another (Rom. 14:1; 15:7), thus destroying the peace, unity, and mutual upbuilding of the congregation.

Why did those "weak in faith" believe that they must be vegetarians and total abstainers and must observe certain days as holy or at least "as better than another" (Rom. 14:5)? Paul presupposes that what they did (or, rather, abstained from doing) was done in faith (Rom. 14:2, 22 f.), "in honor of the Lord" and in gratitude to God (Rom. 14:6). There is no suggestion that the "weak in faith" believed that they were saved by the performance of works of supererogation. The situation in Rome was not that against which Paul had to contend in his letter to the Galatians, nor was it similar to the situation in the church of the sixteenth century against which the Reformers contended. In his *A Shorter Commentary on Romans* (1959), Karl Barth suggests that the "weak in faith" were those who laid hold of these special measures because they did not trust themselves to succeed without these supports, principles, and exercises, and because they feared that without such self-helps they would fall out of grace. Perhaps this is a correct explanation, particularly in view of Paul's sentence about the "failings" (RSV) or "weaknesses" of the weak (Rom. 15:1). But in Rom., ch. 14, Paul does not describe abstinence from meat and wine and the observance of special days as props or self-helps for faith. As we have suggested above, they could have been special signs that some were constrained to set up against the world and a worldly church preoccupied with money, sex, and alcohol.

The situation to which Paul addressed himself in I Cor., chs. 8; 10:23–33, was different and more sharply defined. There it was a case of those whose "knowledge" and "conscience" (lit., "co-knowledge") were "weak" (I Cor. 8:1, 7–11) concerning the existence of God and idols, and who, therefore, refrained from eating food offered in sacrifice to idols. The "weak" believed that "there is one God, the Father . . . and one Lord, Jesus Christ" (I Cor. 8:6). But they had not advanced to the knowledge that—"although there may be so-called gods in heaven or on earth"—"an idol has no real existence," and "there is no God but one" (I Cor. 8:4–5). They believed in God, but they still believed in the existence of idols. Hence, they believed there is still such a thing as food sacrificed to idols (I Cor. 8:7) and that to eat such food would be to be guilty of a syncretistic eating and drinking of the table and cup of the Lord and of demons condemned by Paul himself. "What do I imply then? That food offered to idols is anything, or that an idol is anything? No, I imply that what pagans sacrifice they offer to demons and not to God. I do not want you to be partners with demons. You cannot drink the cup of the Lord and the cup of demons. You cannot partake of the table of the Lord and the table of demons." (I Cor. 10:19–21.)

Whether the "weak" abstain from meat and wine because of an imperfect knowledge of the existence of God, or because such abstinence is a prop to undergird their faith, or because they are constrained to set up special signs of the Christian's freedom from the worship and service of the so-called gods of Mammon and Bacchus, Paul's counsel is the same. He urges everyone, the "weak" and the "strong," to be "fully convinced in his own mind" (Rom. 14:5), to honor and to give thanks to the Lord whether one eats and drinks or not. But his admonition is addressed particularly to the "strong," among whom he classes himself. His own position is: "I know and am persuaded in the Lord Jesus that nothing is unclean in itself" (Rom. 14:14; cf. vs. 20 f.); that "an idol has no real existence" (I Cor. 8:4); and that "the earth is the Lord's, and everything in it" (I Cor. 10:26). But his knowledge is qualified by the law of love (Rom. 14:15). " 'Knowledge' puffs up, but love builds up" (I Cor. 8:1). " 'All things are lawful [in eating and drinking],' but not all things build up. Let no one seek his own good, but the good of his neighbor" (I Cor. 10: 23 f.). Knowledge will pass away, but love never ends (I Cor. 13:8). Here Paul is against Paulinism! Love puts a limitation upon the permission and commandment to eat and drink all things. For love means that we may never by our eating and drinking put a stumbling block or offense in the way of a brother.

But what does it mean "to put a stumbling block or hindrance in the way of a brother" (Rom. 14:13)? What does it mean "to make others fall" (Rom. 14:20) and to "stumble" (Rom. 14:21)? What does it mean for our liberty to "become a stumbling block to the weak" (I Cor. 8:9) and for our food to be a cause of our brother's falling (I Cor. 8:13)?

Ironically, prohibitionists have twisted these passages in Paul's letters to mean that by my drinking I may tempt a man who has a physical or moral weakness for alcohol to drink and thus to stumble and fall, a victim of alcoholism. Paul's meaning is just the opposite! He teaches that he, Paul, who is free to eat and drink, to have a wife, and to earn money (I Cor. 9:4 ff.), may have to abstain—not for the sake of a morally weak brother, but for the sake of the morally strong man who is a vegetarian, a teetotaler, a celibate, and a sabbatarian. The morally strong man, the ascetic, is the man whom Paul calls "weak in faith." Paul is concerned lest precisely those who are morally strong yet weak in faith be caused to stumble and fall by those whose freedom permits them to eat meat, drink wine, marry, earn money, and treat all days alike. To put a stumbling block or offense in the way of a brother is to put something in his way which causes him to fall from his faith that God has accepted him, or which causes him to do something contrary to his faith or conscience.[14]

Tension between "weak" and "strong" parties in Christian congregations has existed down through the centuries and has often resulted in open disruption and schism. In 1935 the writer attended a Presbyterian church in Edinburgh at which two services of the Lord's Supper were held: one at 9 A.M., at which wine was served; one at 11 A.M., at which grape juice was served. I was aghast to see the body of Christ so rent asunder. The "strong" ought to have surrendered their freedom to drink wine for the sake of the unity and peace of the congregation! If and when it becomes widely recognized that the Lord's Table may be furnished with meat, fowl, and fish, and with various beverages, and that it ought not to be restricted to a wafer and a sip of wine, the possibility of the "weak" being offended could be heightened. One hopes that the "weak" will not go so far as to insist that the elements of bread and wine, when blessed, consecrated, and "set apart from a common to a holy use" through prayer by an ordained priest or minister, are necessary for salvation. In that case the "weak" would have to be stoutly resisted for the sake of the confession that Jesus Christ is the *one* Mediator of salvation, the *one* means of saving grace.

Yet some will doubtless still believe that there is a special sacramental value and efficacy immanent in consecrated bread and wine. The "weak" will regard bread and wine as elements in and with which Jesus Christ is realistically, or sacramentally, or spiritually present. They will regard them as "means of grace," as "mediating" salvation, as instruments, channels, or mediators of the Mediator—means by which Christ and his benefits are made available to men. They will esteem "consecrated" elements as "better" or holier than ordinary food. Moreover, the "weak" will ascribe to bread and wine the function of sealing, assuring, and strengthening faith. They will feel that they need them as supports, props, or visual aids to faith. In such a situation both the "strong" and the "weak" will need to hearken to Paul's admonition that they do not judge and despise one another. They will need to acknowledge that both seek to serve, honor, and give thanks to the Lord. It will be especially incumbent upon the "strong" to bear with the failings of the "weak" and not seek to please themselves. The "strong" may not impose their evangelical freedom as a principle binding on others. They may not allow their freedom to become schismatic.

This does not mean that the "strong" are obliged to compromise their faith in evangelical freedom with respect to the Lord's Supper any more than Paul did. They will abide by Paul's sentence: "I know and am persuaded in the Lord Jesus that nothing is unclean in itself" (Rom. 14:14), and that "nothing is to be rejected if it is received with thanksgiving" (I Tim. 4:4). As carefully, patiently, and lovingly as possible they will seek to show their brethren that at the Lord's Table, and then at all meals, they may eat and drink all things.

We pause again to summarize the foregoing. In this second

part of our exposition we have been seeking an answer to the question: *What* may and must men eat and drink with Jesus? We have said that the Lord's Supper was a meal at which the congregation is permitted and commanded to eat and drink not only bread and wine but also fish, fowl, and meat (including pork)—but only as an appeal to the reconciliation accomplished by Christ as the Lamb of God who takes away the sins of the world, and only as an appeal to the blood of the new covenant whereby the dividing wall between Jews and Gentiles has been broken down. We have also said that the Lord's Supper is exemplary of what may be eaten by Christians and all men in their homes and in restaurants. Moreover, we have said that in certain circumstances and for certain individuals the commandment to eat and drink all things includes a freedom to abstain from meats and alcoholic beverages. But after this has been said, the answer to our question is not yet complete. There appears to be an exception to the Pauline dictum that "nothing is to be rejected if it is received with thanksgiving."

There is one thing that is strictly forbidden in both the Old and the New Testament. "You shall not eat flesh with its life, that is, its blood." (Gen. 9:3 f.; cf. Acts 15:20, 29.) "For the life of every creature is the blood of it; therefore I have said to the people of Israel, You shall not eat the blood of any creature, for the life of every creature is its blood." (Lev. 17:14; cf. chs. 17:10, 16; 3:17; Deut. 12:20–28.) Even when the slaughter and eating of animals was permitted, eating the blood and fat of animals was strictly forbidden. The prohibition is "a reminder that the life of another being does not belong to other living beings but to God alone." [15] Also forbidden was the eating of the carcass of an animal that had died of itself (Lev. 11:39 f.) and the flesh torn by beasts (Ex. 22:31; Lev. 17:15 f.). As Calvin rightly perceived in his commentary on Gen. 9:4 f.: "If men should become unrestrained and daring in eating wild animals, they would at length not be sparing of even human blood. . . . The Lord more explicitly declares that he does not forbid the use of blood out of regard to animals themselves, but because he accounts the life of men precious." (Commentary on Genesis; Eerdmans, 1948.) Therefore, cannibalism was absolutely abhorrent. For it not only involved murder but living from the life of another human being. No more frightful judgment could befall men than to be forced in dire distress to eat the flesh of men.[16]

Since eating flesh with its blood is akin to murder, the prohibition against it is really not a contradiction of the Pauline dictum permitting what is received with thanksgiving. For how can a man eat with thanksgiving if he does so at the expense of shedding the blood of a fellowman made in the image of God? How then can he be thankful for the life of his fellowman? It may sound strange to be reminded that Christians may not drink blood or eat that which has been strangled. But it is a matter of the sanctity of human life. Man may eat all things, but he may not commit murder in order to survive. Neither for food, nor for the purpose of acquiring the life, virtues, qualities, and power of the victim, may flesh with its blood be eaten.[17] The Lord's Table is the beginning of the restoration of the peace between man and his fellowman shattered through his sin and fall and symbolized by Cain's slaying his brother Abel. That Table cannot be furnished by robbing and exploiting other men, much less by economic or military warfare against them. "You shall not kill!"

Nevertheless, there is *one* man whose flesh and blood must be eaten and drunk in order that men may live and have eternal life. According to John's Gospel, that man said: "Truly, truly, I say to you, unless you eat the flesh of the Son of man and drink his blood, you have no life in you; he who eats my flesh and drinks my blood has eternal life, and I will raise him up at the last day. For my flesh is food indeed, and my blood is drink indeed. He who eats my flesh and drinks my blood abides in me, and I in him. As the living Father sent me, and I live because of the Father, so he who eats me will live because of me" (John 6:53–57). Jesus' blood is his life and it becomes our life when it is shed. Jesus spoke of his death, of the way in which he would offer up his flesh for the life of the world (John 6:51). He spoke about *how* he must die and about the *effect* of his death. Man will live only through his guilty shedding of the blood of the Son of man. He lives from the once-and-for-all shedding of the blood of the Lamb. Through the sacrifice of his flesh Christ has become the bread of life, not merely for the elect or for believers or for those who participate in the Lord's Supper, but *for the world.* Therefore, men need not and must not eat the flesh and blood of any other man. And therefore all other eating and drinking is a sign, a witness, and a proclamation of the death of Jesus. The secret of *why* and of *what* men may and must eat and drink has been revealed to the congregation. And by the preaching of the gospel and by the Lord's Supper the congregation is to proclaim to all men what and why they may and must eat.

Logically we should now proceed immediately to seek an answer to our third question: *How* may and must men eat and drink with Jesus? How may they do this in remembrance of Jesus and in such a manner that his death is proclaimed until he comes? Unfortunately we are obliged to add an appendix to this second part of our study concerning *what* men may and must eat and drink. We are confronted by the "brute fact" of church history that at least from the time of Ignatius and Justin Martyr down to the present there has persisted a belief in the *mystērion* or *sacramentum* of eating and drinking Christ's body and blood. The belief has been held by all the main branches of Christendom—Eastern Orthodox, Roman Catholic, Lutheran, Reformed, and Episcopalian. Although there has been considerable disagreement among these traditions as to *how* Christ is present in the Eucharist, or Lord's Supper, and as to *how* communicants eat and drink him, all are agreed that Christ is present and is eaten. Those whom we have characterized as the "weak" (although they have been in the vast majority) have long held that in addition to bread and wine, communicants are also repeatedly eating and drinking Jesus' body and blood. Therefore, we must ask whether the commandment to eat all things includes a commandment to eat Jesus. However, rather than interrupt the argument of this book, rather than distract from the positive thesis we are seeking to develop, we have placed our discussion of this question in Appendix I at the back of this book.

3

HOW MEN MAY
EAT AND DRINK WITH JESUS

We have received an answer to our initial question why men may and must eat. God permits and commands men to eat and drink as a sign that Jesus is the Bread of eternal life and the Giver of the water of life whereby men may know and proclaim Christ's death, and in order that men may come to faith. Eating and drinking is the external presupposition of the history of the covenant fulfilled in Christ and the covenant is the internal presupposition of all eating and drinking. In the answer to our second question concerning *what* men may and must eat and drink, we have said that they may eat all things only as an appeal to the reconciliation accomplished in Christ and only as an appeal to the blood of the new covenant whereby the dividing wall between Jews and Gentiles has been broken down and a table fellowship has been made possible among all peoples. We now ask: How may and must men eat and drink with Jesus? We are asking about the goodness of human activity in relation to the divine commandment fulfilled in Jesus.

The general answer that Paul gave is as follows: "Whether you eat or drink, or whatever you do, do all to the glory of God" (I Cor. 10:31). All eating and drinking is to the glory of God! But since the Word and the Spirit have been promised to the church, it may know that the Lord's Supper is to serve God's glory and is to be an exhibition and demonstration of how men may and should eat to the honor of God the Creator, Preserver, Reconciler, and Redeemer of all men.

Paul amplifies what he means by eating and drinking to the glory of God when in the next chapter of his letter to the Corinthians he gives the injunction, "Do this in remembrance of me." We eat and drink to the glory of God when we eat and drink in remembrance of God's Son. *Anamnēsis* means "remembrance" or "recollection." It is distinguished philosophically from *mnēmē* ("memory") as the recalling of an event or of a past impression of an event by a definite act of the will. It consists of (*a*) a recollection in the consciousness or mind, (*b*) a recollection by word, and (*c*) a recollection by act. In this threefold sense anamnesis is a human ethical activity. It is not to be identified or confused with the event or the truth it recalls. In the Corinthian passage anamnesis is not to be identified with God's word and work in Jesus Christ. Although anamnesis occurs in relation to God's activity, it is strictly a human activity and is to be sharply distinguished from God's activity. What God does in Jesus Christ by the Holy Spirit is and remains entirely his action alone. What man may and should do in the face of God's action, that is, by way of recollecting God's action, is and remains entirely man's action. It is sufficient for us to be thankful that there is a firm connection between God's action and ours and that by God's work in Jesus Christ through the Holy Spirit we are made free for a human decision and action. In short, we are made free for anamnesis, and we can be thankful for this without presuming that in, with, and under our work of remembrance (the work of our believing, loving, and hoping, the work of our proclaiming Christ's death) we have to perform the work of God himself. As our human work, anamnesis is the acknowledgment, confession, proclamation, glorifying, and praising of God's work.

It is possible and even likely that when Paul repeated the injunction "Do this in remembrance of me" (I Cor. 11:24, 25), he was thinking of an inward act of recalling to mind or of a recollection in the consciousness. But the verse that immediately follows (v. 26), shows that he was primarily thinking of remembrance as an outward act of proclamation. "For as often as you eat this bread and drink the cup, you proclaim the Lord's death until he comes."

What is meant by this proclaiming? Jeremias and Barrett have suggested that what is meant is verbal proclamation. As the Corinthians ate and drank, the gospel was preached, and thereby the meaning of their eating and drinking was interpreted. This insight is salutary, especially when it is assumed that the act of eating and drinking the elements of bread and wine is in itself proclamatory. The fact is that eating and drinking and food and drink are at best ambiguous and do not necessarily point to Christ and announce him. We perceive the wisdom of the Reformers when they insisted that the preaching of the Word must accompany Baptism and the Lord's Supper, and that the preaching of the Word in the weekly gatherings of the congregation should be accompanied by "the breaking of bread."

Are we confronted by an either/or in the text: either that the Lord's death is proclaimed as often as we eat and drink or that it is proclaimed by the verbal preaching of the gospel? Is it not the thought of the New Testament that Jesus Christ is proclaimed by word and deed? Jesus Christ himself is at once God's word of revelation and work of reconciliation, and his ministry was by word and deed. He was "mighty in deed and word before God and all the people" (Luke 24:19). He not only taught the people but "went about doing good and healing all that were oppressed by the devil, for God was with him" (Acts 10:38). When he sent out the twelve (Matt. 10: 5–8) and the seventy disciples (Luke 10:1–9), he charged them not only to preach that the kingdom of heaven is at

hand, but to heal the sick, raise the dead, cleanse lepers, and
cast out demons. Christ's servants are not only to "teach what
befits sound doctrine" but to show themselves "in all respects
a model of good deeds" (Titus 2:1, 7). With the apostle
James's words ringing in our ears, that faith without works is
dead and that we must be not only hearers but doers of the
word, we conclude that verbal proclamation that is not accompanied by deeds of love and mercy is empty and vain.
Jesus Christ is brought to remembrance when his death is
proclaimed not only by "the foolishness of preaching" but by
the very way in which we eat and drink together with him!
As often as we eat and drink, we proclaim Jesus Christ, not
so much because eating and drinking and food and drink are
signs or symbols of Jesus Christ—though this is certainly true!
—but because we eat and drink together in gratitude and
faith, in love and in hope. Indeed, food and drink cease to be
effective signs of Jesus Christ when they are not eaten and
drunk in gratitude, love, and hope. Then the body and blood
of the Lord is profaned (I Cor. 11:27). We must put far less
emphasis upon the symbolism of bread and wine and inquire
what it means to eat and drink in a "worthy" or appropriate
manner, if we are to understand what it means to proclaim
the Lord's death and what it means to eat and drink in remembrance of him.

Anamnesis occurs as an act of conscious recollection and
of proclamation by word and deed. We stress the fact that it
is an event, an act. It is not brought about by setting up a
static and lifeless symbol such as an image, a painting, a mon-
ument, a gravestone, or a flag. As Jesus Christ is not a timeless
principle or idea but a living, acting, speaking person, so the
recollection of him does not take place by means of static
symbols, not even by means of bread and wine. It occurs in a
history, in an encounter between Jesus Christ and those who
hear and do his word. It occurs in a concrete hearing and
preaching of his word and in the event of eating and drinking

with him. It is an act of the knowledge and acknowledgment of the living, present Jesus Christ.

It follows, therefore, that anamnesis is in no sense an act whereby Jesus Christ is made present, re-presented, realized, and actualized, or whereby his death is reenacted and repeated —as if Jesus Christ had a present existence only in the memory and recollection of Christians, only in the ministry of the church. Jesus Christ as the Lord of space and time is at all times and in all places contemporaneous and omnipresent. There are no times and no places outside his time and his space, for "in him we live and move and have our being" (Acts 17:28). Therefore, all men eat and drink with Jesus whether they hear, believe, and know it or not. Moreover, it is because Jesus is specially present with his congregation by the Spirit that it may recognize and acknowledge his preserving and saving presence. The faith and confession of Christians, their suffering, their prayers, and their works, including Baptism and the Lord's Supper, can attest his presence, but only attest it! They cannot re-present, realize, reenact, repeat, or actualize his presence. Jesus does not become present through our recollection or remembrance; on the contrary, because he *is* present, we may eat in remembrance of him. Although anamnesis occurs in relation to God's action, it is entirely a human activity. Through God's work in Christ through the Holy Spirit we are made free for a human ethical decision and deed. We are free to eat and drink in remembrance of Jesus, without claiming that in, with, and under our work, the work of our believing, loving, and hoping, we also have to do the work of God. Only because Jesus is already present, can there be a proclamation through word and deed by which he is recalled. The cognitive act of anamnesis occurs solely on the ground of his gracious presence. It is not an act by which he is resurrected ever again and given a sort of immortality. (See Appendix II.)

The remembrance of Jesus is not the recollection of a purely past event. It is not the recollection of a dead man, of a man who, like Julius Caesar, lived and died nearly two thousand years ago. It is the remembrance of him "who is and who was and who is to come" (Rev. 1:8) and who "is the same yesterday and today and for ever" (Heb. 13:8). It is the remembrance of him who is at once the crucified Messiah and the risen Lord. Corresponding to the past and present of Jesus, anamnesis is an act of faith and love. So too the act of eating and drinking (together with preaching) is an act of thanksgiving for what Christ has done for us, and an act of love in his gracious presence. Anamnesis embraces, therefore, the twofold form of the ethical response of the congregation to its Lord as an act of faith and love.

Proclamation through word and deed, through the sermon and the common meal, ought not to be conceived as a Socratic maieutic method, which assists at the birth of knowledge, i.e., the recollection of a forgotten but immanent truth.[1] For Jesus is not a truth which is immanent and latent in human consciousness and which, given the proper stimulation, can be vividly recalled to mind. Jesus is the personal truth who is ever and again disclosed to men in his self-revelation through the Spirit. Anamnesis is not the recollection of a past impression of Jesus. It is not as though men, having once acquired a knowledge of Jesus, now possess this knowledge in the recesses of their consciousness, needing only to have it revived and vivified. No, it is a matter of a remembrance of Jesus himself and not of an impression, idea, or experience of him.[2]

How, then, may our eating and drinking be an ethical act in remembrance of Jesus? How must we eat and drink so that it will be a proclamation of his death until he comes? When is it truly a remembrance, a proclamation, a witness, and a confession of him? Eating and drinking is a human act of remembrance when it is an act of faith, love, and hope.

A. An Act of Faith: The Eucharist

Eating and drinking in remembrance of Jesus is an act of faith. Eating and drinking is not faith but is a good work when it is done in faith. Only with the greatest reserve may we say that faith is a spiritual eating and drinking of the flesh and blood of Jesus. Faith will never be able to understand itself as a realization, reenactment, or repetition of the death of Jesus Christ at the hands of wicked men. On the contrary, faith is man's recognition and acknowledgment that Jesus Christ has offered up his flesh as a sacrifice for the life of the world and that all men have been guilty of shedding his blood. In no sense does faith re-present the event of salvation that took place in Jesus Christ. Faith is not the repetition in the lives of those who hear the gospel of what took place once and for all in Christ. The truth and power of faith does not lie in man's existential decision to take up his cross and to die with Christ to the self and the world. Such a view of faith involves an identification of God's redemptive work in Christ with faith as man's work. Faith can only apprehend Jesus Christ as the One who died for us at our hands and rose again. It will not confuse its own human work of decision and response with the dying and rising again of Christ. Much less, therefore, will faith regard the act of eating and drinking as a means by which faith is created or is even strengthened and sustained. "It is quite impossible that the Supper should give faith: for faith must be present before we come" (Zwingli). Faith lives solely from the Holy Spirit as the power of the risen, present Jesus Christ. Eating and drinking is a good work of faith when it points away from itself and bears witness to Jesus as the "author and finisher of our faith" (Heb. 12:2, KJV).

Eating and drinking is preeminently and always an act of thanksgiving for the gift of Christ and the Holy Spirit. Although the noun *eucharistia* is nowhere applied to eating and drinking in general or to the Lord's Supper in particular in the New Testament, it came into common usage in the postapostolic and later periods of church history.[3] As applied to the Lord's Supper it had its origin in the thanksgivings that Jesus offered at the Last Supper (Mark 14:22 f.; Matt. 26:27; Luke 22:17–19; I Cor. 11:24) and perhaps also in the feedings of the multitudes (Matt. 15:36; Mark 8:6; John 6:11). The verb form is synonymous with the word for "bless" generally employed with reference to the blessing, or grace, said before eating. (Cf. Mark 6:41; 8:7; 14:22 and par. and the noun form in I Cor. 10:16.) It is also used of giving thanks for food in Acts 27:35; Rom. 14:6; and I Cor. 10:30. The word "eucharist" or "thanksgiving" ought therefore to be applied primarily to the prayer of thanksgiving offered before and after the meal rather than to the meal itself. If the meal is called a Eucharist, that is, a thanksgiving, then it is so only because it is eaten in gratitude for God's amazing grace. No doubt believers may eat and drink with grateful hearts without always expressing their gratitude with audible prayers. But certainly when the Christian congregation assembles in the name of Jesus to eat and drink it will return thanks with words that can be heard and understood. For as the apostle asks: "If you bless with the spirit, how can any one in the position of an outsider say the 'Amen' to your thanksgiving when he does not know what you are saying?" (I Cor. 14:16). Unless accompanied by prayers of thanksgiving by the congregation, its eating and drinking is not a true Eucharist.

It is well to remind ourselves that not only the Lord's Supper but all works done in the obedience of faith are eucharistic. As the Heidelberg Catechism teaches, good works are works of gratitude. And the apostle exhorts us: "Whatever you do, in word or deed, do everything in the name of the Lord Jesus, giving thanks to God the Father through him" (Col. 3:17; cf. chs. 2:7; 4:2). When the congregation eats and drinks with thanksgiving, it testifies that there are no areas of human life in which we are not to render thanks to God. All life is to be lived in gratitude for his goodness. By the mercies of God we are to present our bodies a living sacrifice, holy and acceptable to God (Rom. 12:1). The writer of the Letter to the Hebrews exhorts his readers: "Through him then let us continually offer up a sacrifice of praise to God, that is, the fruit of lips that acknowledge his name" (Heb. 13:15). Lest it be imagined that a sacrifice of thanksgiving is confined to a verbal confession, the writer adds: "Do not neglect to do good and to share what you have, for such sacrifices are pleasing to God" (Heb. 13:16). When we presently consider eating and drinking as an act of love, we shall see that it is an act in which we do good and share what we have. It is a sacrifice of thanksgiving or a eucharistic sacrifice in both word and deed. Accordingly, Paul tells the Corinthians that they will glorify God by their obedience not only in acknowledging the gospel of Christ but by the generosity of their contribution for others, and that their service will not only supply the wants of the saints but overflow in many thanksgivings to God (II Cor. 9:11–13). Likewise he describes the gifts sent by the Philippians as a "fragrant offering, a sacrifice acceptable and pleasing to God" (Phil. 4:18).

In this sense—but only in this sense—may an eating and drinking in remembrance of Jesus be said to be a eucharistic sacrifice. Christ has presented to God the one atoning sacrifice for sins and also the one true thanksgiving offering. In and through his sufferings he gave thanks to God. There is nothing we can do to atone for sin, nothing we can do to repay God for what he has done for us. A perverted conception of gratitude has crept into some of the church's hymns with the notion that since God has done something for us, we must now do something for him. Such a view of gratitude betrays an ignorance of the situation of the Christian who always remains a debtor to God's grace, always an unprofitable servant. True gratitude consists in recognizing that by nature we are and remain ungrateful and that only in Christ, only by grace are we grateful. Hence the apostle exhorts us to give thanks *in* the *name of our Lord Jesus Christ* (Eph. 5:20), to give thanks to God the Father *through him* (Col. 3:17). He tells the Romans: "I thank my God *through Jesus Christ* for all of you" (Rom. 1:8). The words "by" and "through" are decisive; for only in and by Christ, who has atoned for our ingratitude, can we thank the Father.

Thus eating and drinking is an act of thanksgiving for the grace of creation and preservation. Food and drink are signs that God has created all things and has created them good. (I Tim. 4:3 f.) They are signs that not only Christians but all creatures owe their existence and their preservation to God's benevolence. And as Christians eat and drink they acknowledge that all men have their life as creatures from God. Much more than that: they acknowledge that all men have been created and preserved and have been given food and drink that they may live as God's partners in a covenant of grace. Moreover, eating and drinking is an act of thanksgiving for the grace of the reconciliation of the whole world. It is a sign that Jesus is the bread of life *for the world* (John 6:33, 51), that Jesus is indeed "the Savior of the world" (John 4:42). If the church were to imagine that she ate and drank only for herself or gave thanks only for her own salvation, how could she be a messenger of glad tidings for all mankind? How could she rejoice in her own salvation unless she rejoiced in a salvation wrought for all mankind? As Jonah was chosen, called, judged, and delivered only for the sake of God's love for the wicked city of Nineveh, so the church has been chosen, called, judged, pardoned, and redeemed only for the sake of God's love for a lost world. The salvation for which the church gives thanks in her eating and drinking is the salvation of the world in which her own salvation is included. Not otherwise is her eating and drinking eucharistic!

Eating and drinking is an act of thanksgiving not only for

the salvation of the world in the death of Jesus but for the revelation and manifestation of that salvation in his resurrection from the dead. As the congregation eats and drinks it gratefully recalls that God raised Jesus "on the third day and made him manifest; not to all the people but to us [the apostles] who were chosen by God as witnesses, who ate and drank with him after he rose from the dead" (Acts 10:40–41). In the resurrection of Jesus the apostles beheld the glory of the Word that was made flesh for the salvation of the world. They beheld the kingdom of God coming in power, a new creation, a new heaven and a new earth. In the risen Christ the disciples saw what at the last day will be manifest to all, that in the resurrection sin, death, the devil, and hell have been destroyed.

> The strife is o'er, the battle done;
> Now is the Victor's triumph won;
> Now be the song of praise begun, Alleluia!
>
> The powers of death have done their worst,
> But Christ their legions hath dispersed;
> Let shouts of holy joy outburst, Alleluia!

Each time Christ's followers gather together on the first day of the week it is an Easter celebration. It is a service of thanksgiving and praise because death has been swallowed up in victory. To proclaim the Lord's death until he comes—as often as they eat the bread and drink the cup—is to proclaim his triumphant death revealed and declared in his resurrection.

> The day of resurrection, Earth, tell it out abroad;
> The Passover of gladness, the Passover of God!
> From death to life eternal, from earth unto the sky,
> Our Christ has brought us over with hymns of victory.

Eating and drinking is an act of thanksgiving not only for the salvation of the world accomplished in Jesus' death and revealed in his resurrection but for the living presence of the crucified and risen Lord in the Spirit. By the manifestation, the epiphany, or parousia of Jesus in the form of the Spirit, that is, in the power of Christ's resurrection, the congregation rejoices in the knowledge that it eats and drinks in fellowship and communion with the same risen and glorified Lord Jesus with whom the disciples ate and drank after he rose from the dead. Their eating and drinking becomes a participation, a koinonia, in the body and blood of Christ (I Cor. 10:16). Their table fellowship was a eucharistic fellowship. We shall have more to say about the koinonia when we discuss eating and drinking as an act of love. Our point here is that the congregation eats and drinks in gratitude for the fellowship that has been granted it by the Spirit.

Finally, eating and drinking is an act of thanksgiving not only for Christ's death and resurrection and not only for his presence where two or three are gathered together in his name but for the hope of glory. The congregation eats and drinks in anticipation of eating and drinking when Jesus will appear in glory at his parousia at the end of time. It waits for and earnestly desires "the coming of the day of God" (II Peter 3: 12). And the presence of the Spirit is just the pledge, guarantee, and firstfruits of our inheritance and of our ultimate redemption (Rom. 8:23; II Cor. 1:22; 5:5; Eph. 2:13 f.; 4:30). We shall return to this theme in the final section of this chapter when we deal with eating and drinking as an act of hope. Meanwhile we stress that eating and drinking is an act of thanksgiving for what God has done, does, and will do in Jesus Christ for the creation and preservation, reconciliation and redemption of the world. It is first and last a eucharistic meal in remembrance of Jesus who is the same yesterday, today, and forever. As an act of faith, love, and hope it is always an act of unceasing gratitude.

Precisely as an act of thanksgiving, eating and drinking is an act of repentance. Because God's kindness is meant to lead us to repentance (Rom. 2:4), repentance follows thankfulness or rather is included in it. In the knowledge of what God has mercifully done for us in his Son through the Holy Spirit we know the depth of our sin and misery. In gratitude for everything that has taken place for our good, we acknowledge our sin and guilt. We confess that we have sinned against heaven and before our heavenly Father and are no more worthy to be called his sons (Luke 15:18, 21), not worthy to have Jesus come under our roof (Luke 7:6; Matt. 8:8). In thankfulness for God's gracious turning to us we turn from our evil ways to him and are converted. Grateful that we may eat and drink with Jesus, who accepts us just as we are "without one plea," we eat and drink as penitent sinners. No one ever has, no one ever can make himself worthy to sit at the Lord's Table— not even by his confession of sin. We remain sinners whom Jesus "receives" (Luke 15:1–2) and pardons.

The parable of the prodigal son (Luke 15:11–32) has much to teach us concerning the ways in which men eat and drink, though it is seldom considered in this light. The parable is told with a view to the "publicans and sinners" who drew near to Jesus to hear him and whom he receives and with whom he eats (Luke 15:1–2)—in contrast to the Pharisees and scribes who were offended by such action. In the parable the latter correspond to the elder brother who was "angry and refused to go in" to the feast though his father entreated him (Luke 15:28). They are the "righteous persons who need no repentance" (Luke 15:7) and who feel justified because all along they have served God and kept his commandments (Luke 15:29). Perhaps there is also an implicit contrast between Israel which excludes itself from the Messianic feast and the Gentiles who turn to the gospel, who "will come from east and west, and from north and south, and sit at table in the kingdom of God" (Luke 13:29). But there is no explicit mention of this in the parable.

The main figure in the parable is the younger son, who greedily and arrogantly demands that the father give him the share of the property that falls to him. The father divided his living between the brothers, literally the means of subsistence, the means by which men eat, drink, and live. The younger takes his share, leaves his father, and squanders his wealth in debauchery with harlots (Luke 15:30). It is a picture of a man who in a wild freedom seeks carnal pleasure in gluttony, drunkenness, and fornication. The world used to describe how he lived—*asōtōs* ("loosely," Luke 15:13)—includes the notion of an eating and drinking that is selfish and dissolute, eating and drinking as an end in itself and therefore self-destructive. It is the direct opposite of a thankful and penitent eating and drinking. When his property is exhausted and a famine comes upon the land, the son is glad to feed on the husks that belonged to the swine he was charged to feed, for "no one gave him anything." That, too, is a form of eating and drinking which is the opposite of a joyful meal: it is an enforced fast unto death.

What is portrayed here is "the way of man in his breaking of the covenant with God—the way of lost Israel, of the lost 'publicans and sinners,' of the lost Gentile world." [4] It is a parable of the sin and misery of fallen man, who refuses to live as a creature in dependence upon God's grace and who wants to be "like God," to be his own lord and savior. It is a parable of man who eats of the fruit of the tree of the knowledge of good and evil, so that he may be wise, virtuous, holy, and righteous in himself. And God "gives to all men generously and without reproaching" (James 1:5). The Father who is in heaven "makes his sun rise on the evil and on the good, and sends rain on the just and on the unjust" (Matt. 5:45). Man, however, uses the Creator's bounty, not in the service of God and his fellowman, but in a selfish satisfaction of the lusts of the flesh. He is not grateful but self-serving, not humble but proud.

According to the parable, the prodigal son, perishing from hunger, comes to himself and remembers how many of his father's hired servants have bread enough and to spare. He resolves to return to his father with a confession of his sin and, acknowledging that he is no more worthy to be called a son, to beg to be treated simply as one of the hired servants. He carries out his resolves and starts out on his journey back home. But the father sees him while he is still a long distance off, has compassion upon him, runs to meet him, embraces him and kisses him—"and all this before he has even uttered his confession and request, let alone proved them by corresponding actions of amendment" (Barth). Not only that; he gives orders to clothe his penitent son with the finest robe, to put a ring on his hand and shoes on his feet, to kill a fatted calf for a great feast with music and dancing. They were to eat and be merry.

What is portrayed here is the way back of sinful, dying man to the heavenly Father, his conversion in repentance and sorrow. He makes no claims upon God's grace on the ground of any merits or virtues. We have a picture, too, of how God receives and accepts sinners without any reservations or hesitation and of how there is joy in heaven over one sinner who repents (Luke 15:7, 10). "For this my son was dead, and is alive again; he was lost, and is found." (Luke 15:24.) And what do we have here but a beautiful parable of the way in which this rejoicing is signalized, namely, of the third and perfect form in which men may eat and drink with Jesus? It is a joyous banquet attended by men who were dead in sins and trespasses and by God's omnipotent grace have been raised to newness of life in Christ Jesus. It is an act of thanksgiving for the manifestation of the power of grace in the lives of men who in contrition confess:

> Mine is the sin, but thine the righteousness;
> Mine is the guilt, but thine the cleansing blood;
> Here is my robe, my refuge, and my peace,—
> Thy blood, thy righteousness, O Lord my God.

The Christian congregation's eating and drinking in remem-

brance of Jesus is a celebration. In our day the word is over-
worked and tends to be secularized. But what is it but a celebration of the love of God, the grace of our Lord Jesus Christ
and the communion of the Holy Spirit by thankful and re-
pentant men and women—a celebration that is an echo on
earth of the purer praise and rejoicing of the angels in heaven?

If according to the witness of Holy Scripture the dominant
characteristic of the congregation's eating and drinking is one
of thanksgiving and joy, we are bound to ask why this note is
missing from the observance of the Lord's Supper in most of
our churches. It is a solemn affair marked by sad, mournful, even
morbid thoughts associated with death. It is more like a fast
than a feast. It bears little resemblance to the banquet which
the father prepared for his lost son. It seems that we can no
longer partake of food with glad and generous hearts, praising
God and having favor with all the people, as the first Christians did (Acts 2:46 f.). Could the root cause of our gloomy,
melancholy services be due to the fact that we have lost the
sense of the presence of the risen, living Lord and the sense of
his imminent return? Is it because we think we are commemo-
rating the death of a religious hero in order to make his presence somehow real for us? Or is it because we are materially
and spiritually too rich and too full that we can no longer
know the blessedness of the poor, of the hungry and thirsty, of
those who weep and who are persecuted? If such be the case,
what can we do but cry out, "Come, Creator Spirit," that he
may reform the form and character of our church services?

It is the custom in most of the churches in the United States
and Canada to "celebrate" or "administer" the Lord's Supper
in an austere religious atmosphere in the church sanctuary (a
holy place) and then have a coffee hour or a potluck supper
in the church parlors for fellowship and a social get-together.
In the New Testament such a separation would have been unthinkable. The early Christians did not come together merely
to eat and drink. They did not gather for a purely social affair,

though it was at the same time a social affair! They devoted themselves to four inseparable actions: the apostles' teaching, fellowship, breaking of bread, and prayers. Only when these four elements are combined is the eating and drinking of the congregation distinguishable from the eating and drinking of a group of people in a restaurant, at a political banquet, at a service club luncheon, or at a social function such as the celebration of a birthday or an anniversary. The whole purpose of the fourfold "devotion" of the early Christians was to "praise God," and this is what made it an extraordinarily happy occasion.

Eating and drinking in remembrance of Jesus will be an act of thanksgiving and joy when it is accompanied by the reading and exposition of Scripture. Without the preaching and teaching of the Word, the meaning and purpose of the meal will be ambiguous. It must be accompanied by the oral proclamation of the gospel *and* the law. Otherwise the sermon will degenerate into a moralistic harangue or a quietistic homily. How can God's people partake of food with joyful and single-hearted praise, if the good news of deliverance for the captives is not preached?

Secondly, eating and drinking in remembrance of Jesus will be a genuine Eucharist only when accompanied by "supplications, prayers, intercessions, and thanksgivings . . . for all men, for kings and all who are in high positions" (I Tim. 2:1 f.). A priestly service of the church is to give thanks to God on behalf of those who have never known, or who have forgotten, that they may and must be thankful. The congregation gives thanks not only for what God has done for his elect or for believers but for the whole creation. When thanksgivings and intercessions for politicians and judges; for leaders in finance, commerce, and labor; for educators, authors, reporters, and news commentators; for scientists, artists, and entertainers are missing, the church tends to become a sect. The Lord's Supper is eaten for the private enjoyment of the members rather than as a testimony of the message of grace for all men.

Thirdly, eating and drinking will be an act of thanksgiving when the members of the congregation are "addressing one another in psalms and hymns and spiritual songs, singing, and making melody to the Lord" with all their hearts (Eph. 5:18 f.). May such singing be accompanied by instrumental music and dancing, as at the feast for the prodigal son? Yes, when they accompany the singing of *words* of praise and do not become purely aesthetic acts in themselves. The writer has seen black Christians in Africa and America, their faces wreathed in smiles, clapping their hands and dancing in the aisles as they embraced one another and sang hymns of praise to the Father, Son, and Holy Spirit. They were not conscious of performing any symbolic acts or of dramatizing the history of salvation. They were simply and naturally giving expression to their rejoicing in the Lord in the hymns they sang. When the Puritans banished organ music, the dance, candles, vestments, processions, etc., from their worship of God, they rightly stressed that worship is to be in and by the spoken word. (They compared such things to a speaking in tongues which is not for edification.) But in their emphasis upon the word they eliminated the natural and spontaneous response which the word evokes. Perhaps we can learn from our black brothers and sisters how to make melody to the Lord without developing sophisticated theories about aesthetics, symbolism, and religious drama. Perhaps we can learn to sing and play as little children do. We will avoid artificially contriving art forms; we will do what comes naturally. Thus our eating and drinking will become a sacrifice of praise and thanksgiving.[5]

We have been speaking particularly about the Lord's Supper as a Eucharist, about how it is an act of thanksgiving. If the secret of all eating and drinking has been revealed in Jesus Christ through the Holy Spirit to his congregation, then the

Lord's Supper is an exhibition and demonstration not only
of why and what all men may eat and drink but also of *how*
they are to eat and drink. The Lord's Supper is the model and
criterion of all meals. We have now said that the Supper testifies that all eating and drinking is to be eucharistic. This is not
to say that every meal is a Lord's Supper. It is to say, however,
that the Supper is to inform and illumine eating and drinking
in general. This does not mean that all meals are to be accompanied by prayers of thanksgiving, the reading of the
Word, and singing. But it does mean that all meals are to be
eaten "with glad and generous hearts." Christians will bear in
mind that whenever and wherever they eat and drink, whether
it be in the home or in a restaurant, whether the occasion be a
coffee break or a cocktail hour, it is to be done to the glory
of God and in remembrance of Jesus. It is to be eucharistic.

The consciousness of the connection between the Lord's
Supper and all other meals will find tangible expression in the
way in which Christian families will eat in their homes. Grace
will be said at all meals, not in a perfunctory way, but as a
recollection of the Lord's Table and of all that it declares
about why, what, and how men are to eat and drink. Perhaps
if in our congregations the Lord's Supper could once again
become a joyous banquet of thanksgiving, love, and hope,
Christian families might learn to set aside one meal in the day
when there would be prayer, the reading of God's Word, and
the singing of a hymn. They might manage to do it quite naturally and unpietistically.

The Lord's Supper is a testimony to the gratitude in which
all food is to be eaten. But Christians will not be surprised
when they find expressions of gratitude among those who have
never heard of the gospel or of the Lord's Supper, and therefore do not know him to whom they owe everything. According to Acts 14:16 f., God "did not leave himself without witness" even when he allowed the nations "to walk in their
own ways" and in ignorance of the living God. He did good

and gave them rains and fruitful seasons, satisfying their hearts with food and gladness. The unfeigned gratitude of "the children of the world" will often put to shame "the children of light."

B. An Act of Love: The Agape

Eating and drinking in remembrance of Jesus is an act of love. There can be no genuine Eucharist in our congregations if it is not at the same time an Agape feast. If it is Eucharist, it is Agape; if it is Agape, it is Eucharist. If it is an act of faith, it is an act of love. The two are inseparable. Without love there can be no genuine act of faith and repentance, of thanksgiving and praise, no eating and drinking in remembrance of Jesus, no true proclamation of his death. If the Eucharist is not Agape, then it is eaten "in an unworthy manner." To eat thus is to profane the body and blood of the Lord (I Cor. 11:27). It is to despise the church of God and to humiliate those who have nothing (I Cor. 11:22). Unquestionably we have reached the truly critical point in any ethical interpretation of eating and drinking with Jesus. At this point we are bound to raise the most serious questions concerning the churches' doctrine and practice of the Lord's Supper, namely, concerning the separation of Agape and Eucharist very early in the history of the church.[6] It is a question that also has to be put regarding Zwingli's nonsacramental interpretation. For although he stressed that the Supper is an act of faith and thanksgiving, he neglected to show that it is also necessarily an act of love and of hope.

What is involved in the unity and togetherness of Eucharist and Agape is the teaching of Paul concerning the relation of faith and love and the teaching of James concerning the relation of faith and works. According to Paul, the faith that avails, as opposed to the circumcision of the Jews and the uncircumcision of the Gentiles, is "faith working through love"

(Gal. 5:6). Karl Barth wrote: "Paul never even dreamed of the kind of *pistis* envisaged and criticised in James 2:14–26—the faith which has no *erga*, which is inactive, which does not amount to anything more than a mere knowledge, and which is rightly described by James in v. 26 as without spirit and therefore dead. Indeed, he did not even consider this kind of faith as an alternative. There is no other faith than that 'which worketh by love.' " [7] Hence Paul can say, "If I have all faith, so as to remove mountains, but have not love, I am nothing" (I Cor. 13:2) and James can say, "Faith by itself, if it has no works, is dead" (James 2:17). And the example of works which James specifically mentions is giving the things needed for the body to a brother or sister who is "ill-clad and in lack of daily food." If faith may be defined as "the act of a pure and total reception" of the grace of God and love as "an act of self-giving" corresponding to the self-giving love of God (Barth), then faith and love are two distinguishable but indivisible elements of the Christian life. The unity of faith and love is the basis of the unity of Eucharist and Agape, of thanksgiving and love, in the one act of eating and drinking in remembrance of Jesus.

It goes beyond our purpose to set forth anything like a full-orbed teaching about love, much less to make the necessary distinctions and connections between the three types of love: *agapē, erōs,* and *philanthrōpia.*[8] Nevertheless certain things must be affirmed about the nature of love if we are to acquire a proper understanding about eating and drinking as an act of love. We are speaking about love as a human action in obedience to the first and second commandments to love God and one's neighbor, upon which all the law and the prophets depend (Matt. 22:34–40; Mark 12:28–34; Luke 10:25–28), and which is therefore the fulfilling of the law (Rom. 13:9; Gal. 5:14; James 2:8). We are not speaking about a divine love in us, as if the Christian were a channel, instrument, or vessel through which the love of God flows, or as if the love required of Christians were a sort of repetition, continuation, and prolongation of the love of God. In I Cor., ch. 13, Paul is not describing the love of God in us; he is describing the "more excellent way" which the Christian may and must follow in response and in conformity to the love of God in the grace of Jesus Christ through the fellowship of the Holy Spirit (II Cor. 13:14). Eating and drinking as a work of love is therefore no more a means or channel of the love of God than it is of the grace of God.

While there may be no confusing or mixing of divine and human love, neither may there be a separation of the two. For the basis of the love required of Christians is just the love of God. "We love, because he first loved us." (I John 4:19.) We love because the love of God frees us for love. Man never can take the initiative in love. "For love is of God, and he who loves is born of God and knows God. . . . In this is love, not that we loved God but that he loved us and sent his Son to be the expiation for our sins." (I John 4:7, 10.) "God is love" (I John 4:8)—in his eternal being as Father, Son, and Holy Spirit and in the execution and manifestation of his love in that "God sent his only Son into the world, so that we might live through him" (I John 4:9). The love of God is not what we can know of ourselves about love. "For God so loved the world that he gave his only Son" (John 3:16) and he gave his only Son to be a sacrifice for us. God shows his love for us in that while we were yet sinners, while we were enemies, Christ died for us, the ungodly (Rom. 5:6–10). This is the amazing love of Christ that impels or controls us because we are convinced that one has died for all (II Cor. 5:14). Moreover, the basis of Christian love is that "God's love has been poured into our hearts through the Holy Spirit which has been given to us" (Rom. 5:5). By the Holy Spirit the love of God in Christ Jesus becomes operative and effective in us, so that we are liberated to love God, to love the Lord Jesus, and to love our neighbor. Not that the Holy Spirit is a prolongation of the love of God in us! Not that the Spirit takes from us our own human responsibility and activity! On the contrary, the Spirit sets us free for an act of human love that corresponds and responds to the love of God.

Analogous to God's act of giving himself in his only Son, Christian love is an act of self-giving. As the love of God in the history of Israel and in Jesus Christ is not a mere attitude or emotion but an electing, cleansing, and redeeming act or series of acts, so Christian love does not merely think and feel and will. Naturally it does think, feel, and will. Otherwise it would not be the love of a real man. Love acts. It goes beyond the inwardness of a disposition, attitude, or feeling and becomes an act of love. "Let us not love in word or speech but in deed and in truth" (I John 3:18). As God "gives to all men generously" (James 1:5), he "loves a cheerful giver" (II Cor. 9:7). Hence "it is more blessed to give than to receive" (Acts 20:35). Love for God is an act of complete surrender of the self. It is an act in which the Christian loses his life to become a living sacrifice in service of God. Obviously it is an act of which no man is capable. It is possible only because "I, with body and soul, both in life and in death, am not my own, but belong to my faithful Savior Jesus Christ" and because "by his Holy Spirit he also assures me of everlasting life, and makes me willing and ready in heart to live unto him" (Heidelberg Catechism, Question 1).

Although the first and great commandment is to love God, it is inseparable from the second commandment, to love your neighbor as yourself. "If any one says, 'I love God,' and hates his brother, he is a liar; for he who does not love his brother whom he has seen, cannot love God whom he has not seen." (I John 4:20.) Although love for God is not identical with or exhausted in a love for the neighbor, it is confirmed and becomes visible in love for the neighbor. "God's love evokes the love of the Christian for him, and the two together the mutual love of Christians" (Barth). Barth stresses that the mutual

love of Christians becomes a reality and is exhibited in the
koinonia of the church. It is much more than a love for one's
fellowman. It is much more than a humanistic and humani-
tarian love. It is a love created by the Holy Spirit among those
who know one another as pardoned and sanctified sinners. By
their love for one another, bearing one another's burdens, they
are distinguished from the world. "By this all men will know
that you are my disciples, if you have love for one another."
(John 13:35.) Yet Christian love is not restricted to fellow
Christians. For Paul prays that the Thessalonians may
"abound in love to one another and to all men" (I Thess. 3:12)
and admonishes them: "See that none of you repays evil for
evil, but always seeks to do good to one another and to all"
(I Thess. 5:15). As Jesus prayed for his enemies on the cross
(Luke 23:34), so he commands his disciples: "Love your enemies, do good to those who hate you, bless those who curse
you, pray for those who abuse you. . . . If you love those who
love you, what credit is that to you? For even sinners love those
who love them. . . . But love your enemies, and do good, and
lend, expecting nothing in return" (Luke 6:27–28, 32, 35; cf.
Matt. 5:43–48; Rom. 12:14). Christian love is self-giving, first
to the Lord (II Cor. 8:5), then to the brother, then to all
men. It is not an abstract love for mankind in general; it occurs
in a concrete encounter with the neighbor, even when the
neighbor assumes the form of the enemy for whom Christ
died.

If we have acquired a clearer understanding of the nature of
love required of Christians, we may now understand the Lord's
Supper as Agape, as an act of love. In practice, self-giving includes many kinds of giving—the giving of money, time, and
talents. In the Lord's Supper it is concretely a question of the
giving and receiving of food and drink, of sharing the Lord's
Supper, as a proclamation of the Bread of life. It is not a matter of setting up a symbol or token of our love for one another
by means of a morsel of bread and a sip of wine. Symbolism

and tokenism have been the destruction of genuine Christian fellowship. It is a question of the performance of an ethical act, of a work of love, by sharing food, especially with the poor and outcast. Only as it is an *act* of love, and not a "bare sign" of love, is it a proclamation of the Lord's death and of the love of God.

Scholars have tried—artificially we believe—to distinguish and even to separate the Lord's Supper from the common meal in I Cor., ch. 11, and from the last Passover meal in the Synoptic Gospels.[9] Even if such a distinction could be established on the basis of textual criticism, it cannot be denied that the Lord's Supper took place in the context of a meal. Nor can it be denied that, as far as Paul was concerned, when the meal was eaten in such a way that "each one goes ahead with his own meal, and one is hungry and another is drunk" (I Cor. 11:21), *"it is not the Lord's Supper that you eat"* (I Cor. 11:20). Then one eats and drinks improperly or "in an unworthy manner" (I Cor. 11:27, 29), not because one fails to discern or perceive the body and blood of Christ in the elements, but because one despises the church of God and humiliates the poor who have nothing (I Cor. 11:22). Thus is one "guilty of profaning the body and blood of the Lord" (I Cor. 11:27). Paul is angry and speaks with unusual sharpness, an anger begotten of his tremendous concern for the truth of the gospel and his love of the Corinthians. He says: "I must mention a practice which I cannot commend: your meetings tend to do more harm than good" (I Cor. 11:17, NEB). Paul was saying: It were better that you did not come together at all if you are going to eat and drink the way you have been doing. It were better for you to stay at home and eat there (I Cor. 11:22, 34). Paul is echoing the words of the prophet Amos: "I hate, I despise your feasts, and I take no delight in your solemn assemblies" (Amos 5:21).

How did Paul combat this perversion of a proper eating and drinking of the meal in the meetings of the Corinthian con-

gregation? He reminded them of a tradition he had received
from the Lord, presumably in the church at Antioch which
had sent him forth. He reminded them of that dark night in
which Jesus was betrayed, for that same darkness had now
fallen upon the Corinthian church! He was being betrayed
afresh! More important, he reminded them of the light that
shone in the darkness. That is to say, he reminded them that
bread broken, given, and shared points to him who is the true
bread from heaven and who became the bread of life for the
world by offering up his flesh on the cross. Moreover, the cup
is a sign of the new covenant established through his blood.
Consequently as often as we eat together we preach or proclaim his death for all mankind and as often as we drink
together we call to remembrance not a dead but a living Lord.
On the other hand, anyone who eats the bread and drinks the
cup of the Lord in an unworthy manner, that is, in pride and
lovelessness, sins against the body and blood of Christ. And
in so doing he, like Judas Iscariot, gives up that which is the
only hope of his own salvation.

Paul is able to put the same thing in another way. It is a
matter of distinguishing or discerning the Lord's body. In the
past this has been understood to mean that one has to distinguish the elements of the Lord's Supper from ordinary food.
Now the Corinthians had been doing that only too well. They
valued it as a religious, sacramental sedative, a means of quiet-
ing their consciences while profaning the body and blood of
the Lord by their lovelessness. To discern the Lord's body
means to recognize the church as his body for which he died
and fellow Christians as members one of another in him. "Because there is one bread, we who are many are one body, for
we all partake of the one bread." (I Cor. 10:17.) There is not
more than one body of Christ—e.g., the historical, in which
he died; the "mystical," his congregation; and then a sacramental body in which Jesus Christ is said to be present in the
elements of bread and wine. There is one body of the crucified

and risen Christ from whom the church has been taken, from whom it lives and grows. There is no body apart from him. The kerygma, baptism, Lord's Supper, faith, love, and hope of Christians, the word and work of the apostles—none of these organize or constitute the body. That is exclusively the work of Jesus Christ. He who is the Head himself, and who is first the body, constitutes the congregation as *his* body. This he has done as the one who was crucified on Golgotha (Rom. 7:24; Col. 1:22; Eph. 2:16; I Peter 2:24; Heb. 10:10). And it is in the light of the resurrection of Christ and the quickening work of the Spirit that the congregation may hear and know: "You are the body of Christ" (I Cor. 12:27).

However, one must not think that it is the Spirit of Pentecost, the fullness of gifts, the faith quickened by the Spirit, the palpable consequences of the preaching and acceptance of the gospel, still less the sacraments, which make the congregation to be members of this body. The church is, and they *are* this *in Jesus Christ*, in his election in eternity (Eph. 1:4; Rom. 8:29). And they *become* this in the execution of this eternal election in his death on the cross proclaimed in his resurrection from the dead. It is the work of the Holy Spirit to bring the *knowledge* of all this. In this knowledge the church is Christ's body in such a way that her being as his body precedes her knowledge of it. However, where her knowledge follows her being, then a claim is laid upon the congregation to *conform* to her being in Christ. This is precisely what Paul required of the Corinthians not only in their preaching but also in their eating and drinking.[10]

The apostle concludes his discourse with a solemn warning. Anyone who eats and drinks in an "improper" way, anyone who does not discern the body, "eats and drinks judgment upon himself" (I Cor. 11:29). Lest anyone should think that this judgment is some distant, otherworldly judgment, Paul tells the Corinthians that it is having its effects in their lives. "That is why many of you are feeble and sick, and a

number have died" (I Cor. 11:30, NEB)—not because of a
failure to recognize Christ's body and blood in the elements
as a sort of divine medicine but because of self-righteousness
and lovelessness. Perhaps a psychiatrist might say that these
perverse attitudes have harmful psychosomatic effects in people. Regardless of the truth of a scientific explanation and the
well-known fact that a selfish and joyless eating and drinking
can be injurious to one's health, Paul sees the outward effects
of God's judgment related to a profanation of Christ's death
and to a despising of his holy church. "But if we judged ourselves" (I Cor. 11:31; the same Greek word is used for "discerning the body" in I Cor. 11:29), that is, if we truly saw
ourselves as members of Christ's body, "we should not be
judged" (I Cor. 11:31).[11] "But when we are judged by the
Lord, we are chastened." (I Cor. 11:32a.) "For the Lord dis-
ciplines [or chastens] him whom he loves." (Heb. 12:6 f.)

But thanks be to God: His merciful chastisements are not
final or absolute. He still grants us time. They are laid upon
us in order "that we may not be condemned along with the
world" (I Cor. 11:32). He grants us time to examine ourselves
(I Cor. 11:28) and to change. "Therefore, my brothers, when
you meet for a meal, wait for one another. If you are hungry,
eat at home, so that in meeting together you may not fall under judgement." (I Cor. 11:33–34, NEB.)

We have been at pains to establish that the Lord's Supper
was a meal, and that the abuse of the meal by the Corinthians
was the reason that the Lord's Supper could not be eaten in
remembrance of Jesus and as a proclamation of his death. It is
also evident from Acts 2:42–47 that the "breaking of bread"
was a meal which the early Christians ate together and in their
homes. Their love for the Lord Jesus and for one another
found expression in a table fellowship, in a koinonia. The
koinonia was, of course, an inner spiritual reality: they were
"of one heart and soul." But it was not just a spiritual fellow-

ship: it found outward expression in that "no one said that any of the things which he possessed was his own, but they had everything in common" (Acts 2:44; cf. ch. 4:32). It found expression in an economic communism—not forced but voluntary, and not so that all had the same amount, but distribution was made "to each as any had need" (Acts 4:35; cf. ch. 2:45; II Cor. 8:13 f.; 9:7). This inward and outward koinonia then found expression in the "breaking of bread," in sharing a common meal.

It is perfectly obvious that the Lord's Supper in our churches is not such a fellowship. In the first place it is not a meal. The participants do not sit around tables so that they can see one another, talk to one another, and serve one another. The little portions of bread and wine are received individually. The participants either go forward to the "altar" to receive the elements from the priest or minister, or wait for them to be passed around on trays. The Lord's Supper, as practiced in our congregations, is not only loveless but inhuman! Each partakes alone. It is all so impersonal. No one greets his neighbor with a handshake or a "holy kiss." One does not speak to or listen to those about him. There is not even a fellowship in the Word. Usually one man does all the talking. Often one does not even "see" his fellow Christian. And as for serving and helping one another, especially the poor, that's out of the question. Two beggars sharing a crust of bread have more fellowship than Christians at the Lord's Table! Is it any wonder that in many congregations a coffee hour or a church supper will be served where the members and visitors can get to know one another, speak to one another, and to help one another? But this too can be no substitute for a fellowship in the Word with a table fellowship.

We are loath to venture into the field of practical theology. But two practical questions may be faced concerning the location of the Lord's Supper observance and the frequency of its observance, as these bear upon the character of the table fellowship. It seems unlikely that the Lord's Supper, as a congregational meal, could be served in the church "sanctuary" or auditorium unless the pews were removed and replaced by tables and chairs. Fortunately in most of our churches there are fellowship halls provided with kitchens. There it is customary to hold church dinners or "potluck" suppers. Obviously the Lord's Supper should be served in the fellowship hall. The auditorium could be used for purely preaching and evangelistic services, for Christian education purposes, public lectures, organ recitals, oratorios, etc. It might be suggested that the congregation could use the church auditorium for the ministry of the Word and then repair to the fellowship hall for the Lord's Supper. This would not be a satisfactory solution. It would tend to perpetuate the notion that the church service in the "sanctuary" is a religious affair, whereas a meal taken elsewhere is simply a social affair for the nourishment of the physical body. The Lord's Supper, however, is not a meal in remembrance of Jesus if the congregation does not devote itself to "the apostles' teaching and fellowship, to the breaking of bread and the prayers." The Word may be preached and prayers may be offered without the Supper, but the Supper may never be observed without the ministry of the Word.

Ideally the Lord's Supper should be served weekly when the congregation gathers for the public worship of God. The service clubs manage to meet weekly at noon luncheons, and congregations might do likewise. Nevertheless, it may not always be convenient or feasible for a eucharistic Agape to be held weekly, especially for large congregations. The general rule should be that the congregation should "break bread" together as frequently as possible, at least once a month, and not just on special occasions such as an anniversary supper or an annual congregational meeting for business. Incidentally, it is by no means absolutely necessary for the congregation to have its own building. It could meet in a restaurant, hotel, or motel, as the service clubs do. The more the congregation proclaims the Word, sings and prays, and eats and drinks where men and women work and play, eat and drink, the better!

We have deplored the sundering of Eucharist and Agape. Now we must be more precise and insist that the Eucharist is a love feast only as it is *diakonia*—a service of Christ for fellow Christians and the world. *Diakonia*, a service of deeds of love and mercy, is not merely something that Christians may and must do for the poor and needy when they are dispersed in the world. *Diakonia* has its seat in the church service. It is an integral part of public worship. It is the ethical act that complements, attests, and confirms the preaching of the gospel. When it is lacking, the church service is a torso; it is truncated and defective. The root meaning of the Greek word *diakonein* is to wait on table. From this root meaning, *diakonein* and its cognates were used to refer to a service of the physical and material needs of men. The root meaning of *diakonos* was "waiter." Based on the twofold meaning of waiting on table and serving the needy, the word group was used with theological significance in a number of ways. It was used with reference to Christ's service of men (Mark 10:45; Luke 22:27; Rom. 15:8). *Diakonos* was used in connection with service rendered to God (Rom. 13:4; II Cor. 6:4), to Christ (John 12:26; II Cor. 11:23; Col. 1:7; I Tim. 4:6), to the new covenant (II Cor. 3:6), to the gospel (Eph. 3:7; Col. 1:23), to the fellow disciple or to the church as a whole (Matt. 23:11; Mark 9:35; 10:43). Thus *diakonia* was used of the ministry of apostles, evangelists, prophets, etc. (Acts 1:17, 25; 20:24; 21:19; Rom. 11:13; I Cor. 12:5; II Cor. 4:1; 5:18). Wherefore we conclude that whereas one may distinguish a spiritual and physical *diakonia*, and give priority to the former, the two may not be separated.[12]

Diakonia, understood as the relief of the poor by gifts of money or supplies, is in fact an extension of the service rendered by waiters: it is a matter of supplying food and drink by which men live. If the Lord's Supper is the event in which the congregation eats and drinks with Jesus, then it is a *corporate act of diakonia*, of service in and with Christ for hungry men and women. The *diakonoi* who wait on the guests at the Lord's Table do in fact what deacons in particular and all Christians are called to do, namely, to feed the poor and hungry. In the New Testament and in the early postapostolic church "*diakonia* was itself enshrined at the heart of worship. *Diakonia* and *leitourgia* were so indissolubly linked with one another as to be, in effect, two aspects of the one and the same Godward act on the part of the Christian community" (G. W. H. Lampe). Following the church service the deacons visited and ministered to widows, orphans, the poor, and those in prison. Later the Agape and the church's charitable work were separated from the church service. Thereby both suffered. The church service was removed from the world, and its charity became worldly. Yet even when *diakonia* no longer was "enshrined at the heart of worship," it persisted in an Agape meal which, as Lampe observes, was closely related to the Eucharist and "in itself . . . was a rite which combined worship and edification with service to the needy." To it the poor were invited, or a distribution of food was made to them from the food provided. Although the Agape was frequently abused, its primary object was relief for the poor, for the victims of persecution and for those in prison. According to Justin[13] and Ignatius,[14] the deacons still served the Communion to the people. Hippolytus, however, assigned the distribution of the bread to the bishop, and only the administration of the cups to the deacons, and then only if there were not enough presbyters to do this.[15] The deacons continued to distribute bread at the Agape, until it disappeared from the church service altogether. Sacramentalism and clericalism had begun to displace *agapē* and *diakonia*.

From what has been learned about *diakonia*, it is evident that the Lord's Supper, as an act of love, cannot be restricted to baptized members of the body of Christ. The Table of the

Lord may be fenced against "one who bears the name of brother if he is guilty of immorality" and idolatry; but it may not be fenced against immoral and idolatrous unbelievers (I Cor. 5:9–13). Paul counted upon the attendance of unbelievers and outsiders at the gatherings of the church for thanksgiving (I Cor. 14:16, 23–25). As Jesus received and ate with sinners, as the father received the prodigal son before any confession of sin was made, so the church will extend hospitality to sinners and strangers.[16] It will welcome Communists, atheists, skeptics, scoffers, and adherents of other religions, not for the purpose of converting them—which the church can never do!—but simply to share with them the good news about Jesus and the gifts of food and drink he has provided. Gentile Christians, who have come to share in the spiritual blessings of the Jews, to whom they are indebted, will be anxious "to be of service to them in material blessings" (Rom. 15:27), not only to share the Lord's Supper with them, but to succor them when they are discriminated against and persecuted. As Jesus ate with tax collectors, with the rich, and with rulers, so the church will welcome the rich and the mighty. It will not invite them because of what they might be able to do to support the work of the church financially. Love is never cunning and designing. The church, therefore, will not fawn upon the rich or show partiality to them. It will remember the words of James: "If a man with gold rings and in fine clothing comes into your assembly, and a poor man in shabby clothing also comes in, and you pay attention to the one who wears the fine clothing and say, 'Have a seat here, please,' while you say to the poor man, 'Stand there,' or 'Sit at my feet,' have you not made distinctions among yourselves, and become judges with evil thoughts? Listen, my beloved brethren [Note that James still calls such Christians "beloved"]. Has not God chosen those who are poor in the world to be rich in faith and heirs of the kingdom which he has promised to those who love him? But you have dishonored the

poor man" (James 2:2–6). "As for the rich in this world,"
Paul instructs Timothy, "charge them not to be haughty, nor
to set their hopes on uncertain riches but on God who richly
furnishes us with everything to enjoy" (I Tim. 6:17).

Accordingly, Jesus said to the ruler of the Pharisees who had
invited him to dinner: "When you give a dinner or a banquet, do not invite your friends or your brothers or your kinsmen or rich neighbors, lest they also invite you in return, and
you be repaid. But when you give a feast invite the poor, the
maimed, the lame, the blind, and you will be blessed, because
they cannot repay you. You will be repaid at the resurrection
of the just" (Luke 14:12–14). The fellowship of the church
is not based on friendship, blood relationship, color, race, or
social and economic status. It is the fellowship of those who
are spiritually and physically poor and sick. How can the
Lord's Supper be a joyful Eucharist if the congregation does
not include in its *agapē* and *diakonia* the poor who are oppressed by the rich (James 2:6 f.)? Yet even those who oppress the poor, who blaspheme the honorable name by which
Christians are called, and who persecute the church are not
to be excluded from the Lord's Table. For "if your enemy is
hungry, feed him; if he is thirsty, give him drink" (Rom.
12:20).

Although the church is to issue the invitation, "Come, for
all is now ready," to the rich and the mighty, she will not be
surprised if many begin to make excuses. The church has been
instructed by her Lord how difficult it is for a rich man to
enter the kingdom of God. But this very fact will drive the
church to ask, "Who then can be saved?" and to be comforted
by Jesus' answer: "With men this is impossible, but with
God all things are possible"—even the salvation of poor
Christians. The church will remember that God chose not
many wise, powerful, and of noble birth, but the foolish, the
weak, the low and despised in the world, "so that no human
being might boast in the presence of God" (I Cor. 1:26–29).

The poor, too, cannot boast of their poverty; they can boast only of the utterly free grace of God which availed for rich Zacchaeus, who received Jesus joyfully into his house. And when the crowd saw it, they all murmured: "He has gone in to be the guest of a man who is a sinner" (Luke 19:1–10).

From what we have learned about the Lord's Supper as an act of love, as Agape and as *diakonia*, it is obvious that it cannot be an end in itself. It is the source, the fountain, the wellspring of the church's mission into and for the world. What the congregation does in its public gatherings by way of *agapē* and *diakonia* is to be done in and for the world. It is to carry its service of love by word and deed to all men. It is to "go out to the highways and hedges, and compel people to come in" with the mighty compulsion of love that is "patient and kind." The Lord's Supper is not an act of love or of faith, and it is not a genuine Eucharist, if it does not have this outreach. Conversely the church's welfare work will tend to become moralistic and legalistic if it is cut off from its root in the church service where Jesus Christ is known and remembered.

When the church moves out into the world in service to the poor and needy, it does not cease to eat and drink with Jesus. For God in Christ is not only in the church where the Word is truly preached and the "sacraments" are rightly administered, as the Reformers taught. Jesus is first and above all outside our churches and all around our churches, so that when we come out of church we stumble over him (Helmut Gollwitzer). Jesus is with the least of his brethren, as the well-known passage in Matt. 25:31–46 teaches. It is true that God's Son is there where two or three are gathered together in his Name, that is, where he is revealed in the power of his Word and Spirit. But the God who is present and is revealed and is known and confessed in and with his church is none other than Jesus, who is now secretly, but no less really, present in solidarity with the hungry, thirsty, naked, sick, and im-

prisoned people of the world and with those who are strangers
to the household, the church of God. It is noteworthy that
both the righteous and the unrighteous will say: "Lord, when
did we see thee hungry and feed thee, or thirsty and give
thee drink?" (Matt. 25:37; cf. v. 44). Nevertheless, the King
will answer them: "Truly, I say to you, as you did it to one of
the least of these my brethren, you did it to me. . . . As you
did it not to one of the least of these, you did it not to me"
(Matt. 25:40, 45). We will not go so far as to say that Jesus *is*
a hungry, thirsty, naked, sick, and imprisoned human being,
as some theologians have done.[17] Such human beings are his
brothers. But he has so identified himself with them in all
their poverty and distress that we can encounter him only in
them whether inside or outside the church walls. Jesus is with
the poor Lazarus who lies at the gate of us rich Christians,
desiring to be fed with what falls from our tables (Luke 16:19–
31). He is in and with a child whose flesh has been eaten away
by napalm in Vietnam. He is with the refugees fleeing from
their bombed-out villages. He is with a convicted murderer in
death row who is waiting to die in the gas chamber, and he is
with the widow and orphans of the man who was murdered.
He is with a young girl who is a victim of dope. He is with a
whole race that has been kept down and deprived of its rights
because of its color. Yes, God in Jesus is all around us—the
suffering, weeping, oppressed, hungry, and thirsty God who
cries out to us.

Thus once again we perceive that the church cannot make
an absolute distinction between the Lord's Supper and the
eating and drinking of the children of the world. Christians,
moreover, have no monopoly on *agapē* and *diakonia*. They
ought not to forget that it was a godless Samaritan (a modern equivalent might be a Communist) who was neighbor to
the man who fell among robbers and who showed mercy to
him, whereas the priest and the Levite (comparable to Christians) passed by on the other side. The Samaritan not only

bound up the wounds of the man but took him to an inn and paid the innkeeper for his room and board. Shall we deny that the Lord's Supper was secretly eaten in that hotel? Was it not an unconscious remembrance of Jesus, and therefore of *the* neighbor, *the* mercy of God? (Luke 1:78; 10:29–37.)

It is noteworthy that the needs of Jesus in the least of his brethren are all bodily needs. Christendom has often been more concerned about the spiritual needs of men—about their unbelief, false doctrine, and personal immorality; about feeding their souls. Certainly this is the impression that is given by the one-sided way in which the Lord's Supper is eaten in our congregations. Here Jesus, like a thoroughgoing materialist, declares that we will be judged in relation to the bodily needs of the men, women, and children around us. Helmut Gollwitzer quoted the Russian Christian thinker, Nicolas Berdyaev, who once said: "My own bread is only a materialistic question, but my neighbor's bread is a spiritual question." Jesus makes the social and economic question the final criterion of our love of Jesus and of our gratitude for what he has done for us. It is also the criterion of our doctrine and practice of the Lord's Supper. If it is Eucharist it is Agape. It is at once an act of thanksgiving and an act of love in remembrance of Jesus.

Diakonia, service to Christ in the least of his brethren, is also a *political* action. For the hungry, thirsty, naked, sick, the refugees, and imprisoned are representative of large groups in our society. Therefore it is not only a question of giving aid to certain individuals but of helping deprived and underprivileged minorities. The church knows that in the as yet unredeemed world God has appointed the State to provide for justice and peace by means of the threat and exercise of force, according to the measure of human judgment and human ability (Barmen Theological Declaration). The ruler is the *diakonos* and the *leitourgos* (Paul used both words in Rom. 13:4, 6) "for good," that is, for the sake of the poor neighbor. The congregation reminds both rulers and ruled of their responsibility, not only by its preaching, prophetic utterances, and intercessory prayers for "all in authority" (I Tim. 2:1 f.), but by the concern for the poor which it manifests in the Lord's Supper. Moreover, Christians will see their own political responsibility for the establishment of a just state as an extension of the *diakonia* in the congregation. They will not be politically indifferent, apathetic, and neutral. The congregation will work and vote for that party and program which is concerned for peace, for ridding cities of slums and ghettos, for equal rights, and for prison reform. It will resist a "Pilate-state" that perverts justice in order "to satisfy the crowd," not by taking up the sword against that state but by its witness and suffering.

Eating and drinking in remembrance of Jesus is an act of love. We would conclude this section of our study by reminding ourselves that an act of love is an act of *humility*. "Love is not jealous or boastful; it is not arrogant or rude. Love does not insist on its own way." (I Cor. 13:4 f.) This humility is to be reflected in the way in which Christians are to serve one another, that is, in the *ordering* and *conduct* of the Lord's Supper.

It will usually be the case in every congregational meal that someone will be asked to preside. In the early church that person was called a "president." Until he became vested with sacramental powers, he served as a moderator or chairman. There will also need to be those to prepare the meals and wait on tables. They may be called deacons or waiters, for that is their function. But since all are deacons, all are servants, all are ministers, the function should not belong exclusively to some, and certainly should not bestow positions of power, authority, and honor above the others. It cannot be a meal in which one man is the host and the others guests. There is one Host, one Giver of food and drink, who is Jesus Christ. In virtue of his real presence through the Spirit, he needs no

vicar to take his place, no one equipped with special supernatural powers to "administer" or "celebrate" the Lord's Supper for the others. It is not true that the congregation can
eat and drink in remembrance of Jesus only when an ordained
or consecrated bishop, priest, or minister is present. In short,
the un-Biblical distinction between clergy and laity cannot be
definitive for the Lord's Supper. This is not to deny that in the
New Testament there is a plurality and diversity of gifts and
ministries. It is to deny that there is a ministerial *order*, much
less a special sacramental or sacerdotal ministry. Nor is this
to deny that all things are to be done "decently and in order"
in the church. But as the Barmen Theological Declaration,
Art. 4, teaches: "The various offices in the Church do not establish a dominion of some over the others; on the contrary,
they are for the exercise of the ministry entrusted to and en-
joined upon the whole congregation."

The 1972 General Assembly of The United Presbyterian
Church in the U.S.A. adopted the recommendations of its
Special Committee on the Theology of the Call for changes in
the Directory of Worship. We quote from these in part:

> All believers participate in the one ministry of Jesus Christ who
> is at once God's word of revelation and work of reconciliation.
> This ministry represents Jesus' ministry by word and deed
> through the Holy Spirit. Christ is the minister and servant of
> God in whom and through whom the whole Church and every
> member of the Church is called to the one ministry. . . .

> The entire session has responsibility for the whole ministry of
> the congregation and exercises special responsibility for the or-
> dering of the congregation's corporate worship, including ad-
> ministration of Baptism and the celebration of the Lord's
> Supper. While it is the practice in the United Presbyterian
> Church for a continuing member of presbytery to preside at
> the administration of Baptism and the celebration of the Lord's
> Supper, the corporate nature of the Church's ministry means
> that the session and its moderator, with the permission of the

presbytery, have the authority and freedom to invite a member
or members of the congregation to preside on particular occasions within the bounds of that congregation. . . .

The celebration of the sacraments occurs when all the people
celebrate together, rather than receive the gifts through an individual who performs the sacraments for them. For the sake
of order the sacraments are to be administered only by those
duly appointed.

The Committee on the Theology of the Call was not asked
to study the church's doctrine and practice of the Lord's Supper. But it is evident that its recommendations point to a way
of eating and drinking in remembrance of Jesus that is an act
of humility and love.

In order to illustrate how Christians are to serve one another in the performance of the most menial tasks, Jesus
washed the feet of his disciples at the last Passover Supper.
We would not argue for the practice of foot washing in our
churches because it is not a custom in our Western culture.
Doubtless it could have symbolic value. Yet it is doubtful
whether Jesus was interested in instituting a symbol. He took
a common service that was rendered by slaves for their masters
to teach that his disciples should perform the service of slaves
for one another and that among them the distinction between
masters and slaves, rulers and ruled, rich and poor, should no
longer prevail. There would be something artificial about in-
troducing the *pedilavium* into our churches in the West. What
Jesus requires is not *symbols* of our love for one another, but
ethical *acts* of humility and love which will then be authentic
signs that "the Son of man came not to be served but to serve,
and to give his life as a ransom for many" (Matt. 20:28).

The principle of foot washing as practiced in Eastern countries may be retained in the Lord's Supper by Christians
taking turns in waiting on tables and serving one another. It
is significant that Luke locates Jesus' teaching on this point

among the discourses he delivered at the Last Supper. When a dispute arose among the disciples as to which one of them was to be regarded as the greatest or which were to be given the chief seats in his kingdom, Jesus said: "The kings of the Gentiles exercise lordship over them; and those in authority over them are called benefactors. But not so with you; rather let the greatest among you become as the youngest, and the leader as one who serves. For which is the greater, one who sits at table, or one who serves? Is it not the one who sits at table? But I am among you as one who serves" (Luke 22:24–27; cf. Matt. 20:20–28; Mark 10:35–45). The same lesson had been related earlier by Luke. When Jesus was invited to dine at the house of a ruler who belonged to the Pharisees and he noticed how those who were invited chose the places of honor, he said to them: "When you are invited by any one to a marriage feast, do not sit down in a place of honor, lest a more eminent man than you be invited by him; and he who invited you both will come and say to you, 'Give place to this man,' and then you will begin with shame to take the lowest place. But when you are invited, go and sit in the lowest place, so that when your host comes he may say to you, 'Friend, go up higher'; then you will be honored in the presence of all who sit at table with you. For every one who exalts himself will be humbled, and he who humbles himself will be exalted" (Luke 14:7–11). Although this passage and the two following (Luke 14:12–24) contain parables of an eschatological Messianic feast when "the host comes" and repayment is made "at the resurrection of the just" (Luke 14:14), yet surely they are descriptive of how Christ's disciples are required to "eat bread in the kingdom of God." They are to eat and drink in humility as each other's slaves and waiters. This is the order that is to prevail at the Lord's Supper. Christ's followers are not to eat like the Pharisees, who love "the best seat in the synagogues" (Luke 11:43) or the scribes, who love "the places of honor at feasts" (Luke 20:46).

We have been speaking particularly of the Lord's Supper as an Agape meal, and about how it is an act of love. If the secret of all eating and drinking has been revealed in Jesus Christ through the Holy Spirit to the congregation, then the Lord's Supper testifies that all eating and drinking is to be an act of love, of fellowship, of sharing one's daily bread, and of serving the least of Christ's brethren. If the *order* of the Lord's Supper is such that all distinctions of race, color, nationality, sex, and caste; of religion, culture, and education; of economic, social, and political status, are broken down; if it is a Table fellowship at which no one claims that any of the things which he possesses are his own and all are servants and slaves of one another, then the social and political implications of the Lord's Supper are incalculable. The Lord's Supper is, in fact, the ecclesiological basis of social ethics. In the light of the Agape meal must not a Christian be committed to democracy and socialism? The question is being warmly debated in Europe. This much is certain: an economic and political system in which equal rights for all citizens are violated, in which the poor are exploited by the rich, and in which large groups are discriminated against and oppressed by reason of their color or religion, is in flagrant contradiction of the Lord's Supper. But the immediate question before us is whether the church will be able to render the social and political witness it owes to the world without a radical reformation of its own doctrine and practice of the Lord's Supper.

C. An Act of Hope: The Marriage Supper

It has been established that eating and drinking in remembrance of Jesus is an act of faith and of love. It is at once a Eucharist and an Agape. Jesus is remembered and proclaimed by word and deed, by an act of thanksgiving and love. He is remembered as the one in whom the kingdom of God has come. He is remembered as the one through whom all things were created and preserved and as the one in whom God has reconciled the world to himself. He is remembered as the Giver of food and drink and as the Bread of life. But eating and drinking is also an *expectation* and an *anticipation* of Jesus' coming again. Eating and drinking in the expectation of his coming is an act of hope.

Jesus *came!* He came as the fulfillment of Israel's hope in the promise of the Messiah (Luke 1:31–33, 54 f., 68–79; 2:29–32; John 1:41). "For all the promises of God find their Yes in him." (II Cor. 1:20.) Yet the fulfillment of the promise of the Messiah in the birth and life of Jesus was itself a promise and pledge of a future coming in his resurrection from the dead. He first came incognito—in a weakness and suffering that looked forward to the manifestation of the glory of the crucified Messiah. He first had to suffer many things and be killed and on the third day be raised. Yet the fulfillment of the promise that Jesus would come again in his resurrection was itself a promise that he would come again in the Holy Spirit to his church during the last days. His coming in the Spirit was the pledge, guarantee, and firstfruits of his coming again in glory at the final parousia.

Jesus *is coming!* "Behold, I am coming soon." (Rev. 3:11; 22:7, 12, 20.) "The Lord is at hand." (Phil. 4:5; cf. James 5:8 f.; I Peter 4:7; Rev. 1:3.) To which the congregation responds: "Amen. Come, Lord Jesus!" (Rev. 22:20) and "Maranatha": "Our Lord, come!" (I Cor. 16:22). Eating and drinking is not hope, but it is done in hope when it awaits the imminent return of Jesus. If the congregation does not hope that he will come soon, it does not hope. A deferred hope is a forlorn hope, a vain, disappointed, deluded hope. In the New Testament it is never hope in some remote future. Neither is it the expectation of some dark, unknown future. The congregation hopes for a future which is Jesus Christ and which is therefore known and certain. It hopes in the coming of the Lord who has come. Therefore, it cannot hope without faith that is active in love; it cannot believe and love without hoping. Faith, love, and hope are three forms or modes of a human ethical activity in response to and corresponding to him "who is and who was and who is to come" (Rev. 1:4, 8; 4:8; 11:17; 16:5), who is "the same yesterday and today and for ever" (Heb. 13:8). Eating and drinking with Jesus is, therefore, at once a Eucharist, an Agape, and a Marriage Supper. The Lord's Supper is an eschatological meal "until he comes." It is a Messianic feast of love and joy, eaten in faith in the kingdom that has come and in hope in the kingdom that is coming. It is "the marriage supper of the Lamb"; it celebrates "the marriage of the Lamb [who] has come, and his Bride [who] has made herself ready" (Rev. 19:7–9). The Bridegroom is coming to be united forever with his bride. But every time Jesus comes in the Spirit to eat with his congregation, the Lord's Supper is a blessed antepast, or foretaste. Therefore: "Blessed is he who shall eat bread in the kingdom of God" (Luke 14:15). "Blessed are those who are invited to the marriage supper of the Lamb." (Rev. 19:9.)[18]

It is necessary to understand that the Jesus who is coming in the Spirit and who is coming in power and glory at the last day is none other than he who has come again in his resurrection. As Karl Barth has expressed it: "The New Testament knows of . . . only one new coming of the One who came before, of only one manifestation of His effective presence in the world corresponding to His own unity as the One who came before. This does not exclude the fact that His new coming and therefore His manifestation in effective presence in the world takes place in different forms at the different times chosen and appointed by Himself and in the different relationships which He Himself has ordained."[19] The three forms of the parousia are the resurrection, the outpouring of the Spirit, and the final return of Jesus. Although these three forms must be carefully distinguished, they are forms of one and the same event. The Easter event is the first and basic form in which the glory of the Word that became flesh was manifested and was beheld. The outpouring of the Spirit is the coming of Jesus Christ in the last times which still remain. The parousia in the final stage is the universal, unambiguous and conclusive manifestation of Jesus as the redemption of the whole creation. Since Jesus unquestionably prophesied the manifestation of the kingdom of God with power and the coming of the Son of Man in his kingdom within the lifetime of those around him (Matt. 10:23; 16:28; 26:64), the resurrection was the parousia. With special reference to John's Gospel we may also say that Jesus' promise, "I will come again" (John 14:3, 18, 28) has been fulfilled and is ever and again fulfilled in the outpouring of the Spirit (John 14:16; 15:26; 16:7). Finally, the coming of the Son of Man "as the lightning comes from the east and shines as far as the west" (Matt. 24:27; Luke 17:24) so that all will see the glory of the Lord, is the parousia.

The kingdom of God has come and has been revealed to the apostles in the death and resurrection of Jesus Christ. In his death the end of the world has already taken place. "He has appeared once for all at the end of the age to put away sin by the sacrifice of himself." (Heb. 9:26b.) He has "abolished death and brought life and immortality to light" (II Tim. 1:10). In his resurrection a new heaven and a new earth, a new creation, has emerged and has been manifested. Thus the present time of our world is really the "last days" or "the end of the times" (I Peter 1:20; I John 2:18; Jude 18; II Tim. 3:1; II Peter 3:3; James 5:3; Heb. 1:2; Acts 2:17). They are the "last days" in that the history of Israel, and also world history, have reached their goal in the death of Jesus, and they are the "last days" in that "the form [schēma; lit., the present appearance] of this world is passing away" (I Cor. 7:31; cf. I Peter 4:7; I John 2:17), rushing toward the final and universal manifestation of a new time and a new creation. As theologians have put it: the clock has stopped, but the pendulum still swings. The war is over and peace has been declared, but there are still skirmishes where soldiers have not yet heard the news. Wars, famines, earthquakes, and pestilence are but the death rattles of a dying world. Our world, whether it knows it or not, is living on borrowed time. And those who have become partakers of the Holy Spirit "have tasted ["taste," NEB] the powers of the age to come" (Heb. 6:4 f.).

In the light of the threefold form of the parousia, in the light of the kingdom that has come, now is, and is to come, let us seek to understand eating and drinking as an act of hope, and therefore, as "the marriage supper of the Lamb." Jesus is the Bridegroom who in everlasting faithfulness to the promises of God came to fulfill the one marriage covenant of grace God made with man. When the Word became flesh, God, in the person of his Son, chose to bind himself to man and man to himself irrevocably and indissolubly. The incarnation of the Son of God is *the* marriage, *the* union of God and man; and the resurrection of Jesus Christ was the manifestation, the pronouncement and publication of that marriage. In and with the election of man in Jesus Christ, there is the special election of the one people of God to be his holy bride that she may bear witness among the Gentile nations to God's covenant of grace with all men (Ex. 34:15; Deut. 31:16; Ps. 73:27; Isa. 54:5; Jer. 3:14; 31:31 f.; Ezek., ch. 16; Hos. 2:19 ff.).[20] According to the witness of the Old Testament, Israel was a faithless and adulterous bride. But God remained a faithful husband. Though he punished Israel for playing the harlot, he vowed: "I will betroth you to me for ever; I will betroth you to me in righteousness and in justice, in steadfast love, and in mercy. I will betroth you to me in faithfulness; and you shall know the LORD" (Hos. 2:19 f.). Indeed, he promised through the prophet Jeremiah that he would make a new covenant with the house of Israel and the house of Judah. The covenant that "I will be your God and you shall be my people" is not to be abrogated. But the covenant will be new in that Israel will be faithful as God is faithful. "I will put my law within them, and I will write it upon their hearts. . . . And no longer shall each man teach his neighbor and each his brother, saying, 'Know the LORD,' for they shall all know me, from the least of them to the greatest." Moreover, the newness of the covenant will consist in the fact that God "will forgive their iniquity" (Jer. 31:31–34).

According to the New Testament the fulfillment of the new covenant, or marriage, occurred in "the last days" with the coming of Israel's Messiah and the outpouring of the Spirit (Acts 2:17–21, Rom. 2:14 f.; II Cor. 3:3, 6–18). According to Matt. 9:14–17 (and par.), the Bridegroom has come and therefore Jesus and his disciples, in contrast to the disciples of John and the Pharisees, do not fast. "Can the wedding guests mourn while the bridegroom is with them?" Thus the meals Jesus ate with publicans and sinners and with his disciples, including the feedings of the multitudes, were secretly wedding feasts celebrating the marriage of the Lamb. They were messianic meals in fulfillment of the feasts foretold by the prophets. (Cf. esp. Isa. 25:6–9; 55:1–5; 65:13.)[21] But these meals were anticipations and promises of the messianic meals at which the risen Christ would come again and eat with his disciples in the kingdom of God (Acts 10:41). But first the days must come when the bridegroom is taken away from them and then they will fast. The Bridegroom must first give himself up for his bride, that "he might sanctify her, having cleansed her by the washing of water with the word, that he might present the church to himself in splendor, without spot or wrinkle or any such thing, that she might be holy and without blemish" (Eph. 5:25–27). The post-Easter meals were fulfillments of the promise Jesus made at the last Passover Supper that he would not drink of the fruit of the vine until that day when he would drink it new with his disciples in his Father's kingdom (Matt. 26:29; Luke 22:16, 18, 30).

These post-Easter meals were in turn promises that after his ascension Jesus would ever and again come in the Spirit to eat and drink with his followers during the last times.

The Lord's Supper is truly "the marriage supper of the Lamb." For as often as the congregation eats this bread and drinks this cup it proclaims the Lord's death and therefore the new covenant, the new marriage, in the blood of the Lamb (I Cor. 11:25 f.). But again the Lord's Supper is a promise and foretaste of the final appearing of the Bridegroom in glory. Then the saints will celebrate the marriage of the Lamb "face to face." Then they will *see* what now they can only *believe*, namely, that in Jesus the kingdom has come, the new covenant has been fulfilled, the marriage consummated, and that he himself is the food of eternal life.

If the time of this world is the "last time" between Christ's resurrection and final parousia—the three and a half times, or forty-two months, of the Apocalypse—then all men eat and drink in the "last time," whether they know it or not. Once again we cannot make an absolute distinction between the Lord's Supper and meals eaten by unbelievers. If "the creation waits with eager longing for the revealing of the sons of God," and if "we know that the whole creation has been groaning in travail together until now; and not only the creation, but we ourselves, who have the first fruits of the Spirit, groan inwardly as we wait for adoption as sons, the redemption of our bodies" (Rom. 8:19, 22 f.), then all men eat and drink with eager longing for the marriage supper of the Bridegroom and his bride, when "the creation will be set free from its bondage to decay." To be sure, the world does not know about the great transformation of all history and the cosmos that has taken place in the death and resurrection of Jesus Christ. It does not know about "the revelation of the mystery which was kept secret for long ages but is now disclosed and through the prophetic writings is made known to all nations" (Rom. 16:25 f.). Though the hope of the world is the hope of Israel and the church, the world does not have a "living hope"; it eats and drinks as "having no hope and without God in the world" (Eph. 2:12). The function of the church is to announce: "Come, for all is now ready," and to invite all men, Jews and Gentiles, to come to the wedding feast of the Lord—to a meal of thanksgiving and repentance, of love and hope.

According to the Synoptic meal-parables of the wedding feast given for the king's son (Matt. 22:1–10) and the great feast (Luke 14:16–24), the invitation was first extended to "the lost sheep of the house of Israel" (Matt. 10:5 f.). But "they all alike began to make excuses" (Luke 14:18). Then the king or the householder was angry, and told his servants to go to the thoroughfares and to invite to the marriage feast as many as they could find. "For I tell you, none of those men who were invited shall taste my banquet" (Luke 14:24). The parables agree with Paul's teaching in Rom., chs. 9 to 11, namely, that through Israel's trespass and stumbling "salvation has come to the Gentiles" (cf. Acts 13:46–48; 18:5 f.; 28:23–29). Now the church has also become Christ's bride (II Cor. 11:2; Eph. 5:22; Rev. 19:7 ff.; 21:2, 9; 22:17), but only in virtue of having been grafted into the true olive tree by faith (Rom. 11:17 ff.) and having become "fellow citizens with the saints and members of the household of God" (Eph. 2:19). The Lord's Supper is the fulfillment of the words: "Many will come from east and west and sit at table with Abraham, Isaac, and Jacob in the kingdom of heaven, while the sons of the kingdom will be thrown into the outer darkness; there men will weep and gnash their teeth" (Matt. 8:11 f.; cf. Luke 13:28–30).

Nevertheless, the terrible judgment that has fallen upon Israel as a whole, its exclusion from the marriage supper, is not final and absolute. In the first place Paul teaches that "a hardening has come upon part of Israel" (Rom. 11:25) and that "at the present time there is a remnant, chosen by grace"

(Rom. 11:5). Paul saw in the fact that he himself was an Israelite a proof that God has not rejected his people whom he foreknew (Rom. 11:1 f.). Moreover, he magnified his ministry to the Gentiles in order to make his fellow Jews jealous, "and thus save some of them" (Rom. 11:13 f.).[22] Secondly, the New Testament teaches that the judgment upon Israel as a whole will last only "until the times of the Gentiles are fulfilled" (Luke 21:24) and "the full number of the Gentiles come in." Then "all Israel will be saved" (Rom. 11:25–26). Thus when the congregation sits down at the marriage supper of the Lamb it knows (or ought to know) that its feast is imperfect, not with respect to the presence of the Bridegroom in its midst, but with respect to the absence of the guests who were first invited. So it sings:

> Let Zion's time of favor come;
> O bring the tribes of Israel home;
> And let our wondering eyes behold
> Gentiles and Jews in Jesus' fold.[23]

> Then shall Israel, long dispersed,
> Mourning seek the Lord their God,
> Look on him whom once they pierced,
> Own and kiss the chastening rod.[24]

The fact that we Gentiles have been invited to the marriage supper of the Lamb, and have actually eaten and drunk in the presence of the Lord, is no certain guarantee that we will be accounted the true guests either during this "last time" or at his final parousia. There is a highly critical passage in Luke 13:22–30, where it is written: "Then you will begin to say, 'We ate and drank in your presence, and you taught in our streets.' But he will say, 'I tell you, I do not know where you come from; depart from me, all you workers of iniquity!'" Doubtless the reference is to unbelieving Jews. But it is also applicable to pseudo Christian Gentiles. Did not Paul warn: "You stand fast only through faith. . . . For if God did not spare the natural branches, neither will he spare you" (Rom. 11:20 f.)? According to Rev. 19:7 f., the Bride who made herself ready for the marriage of the Lamb is the Bride to whom " 'it was granted . . . to be clothed with fine linen, bright and pure'—for the fine linen is the righteous deeds of the saints." According to Matt. 22:11–14, when the king looked at the guests and saw a man without a wedding garment, that man was cast into outer darkness. "For many are called but few are chosen"; that is, many will be invited to the wedding feast, but only a few will live and act as those who are the elect of God and Christians. We have seen that such was the case in the Corinthian congregation: many were eating and drinking judgment upon themselves by their self-righteousness and lovelessness.

Matthew, ch. 25, contains three parables, all of which are related to the wedding feast and all of which put to the congregation the critical question whether its present existence in the interim time has really been spent in expectation of the imminent return of the Bridegroom. For the Judge who is standing at the doors (James 5:9) is coming and "will bring to light the things now hidden in darkness and will disclose the purposes of the heart" (I Cor. 4:5) so that "each one may receive good or evil, according to what he has done in the body" (II Cor. 5:10). The last parable, that of the sheep and the goats, which we have already considered, asks whether its eating and drinking has been an act of love for the least of Christ's brethren. The second parable, that of the talents, asks whether the church has been a missionary church, whether it has been diligent, according to the measure of grace granted to it, in sharing the gospel of the kingdom with others. However, unless we are mistaken, the first parable, that of the wise and foolish maidens, raises the basic and crucial question. The answer to it determines whether the church is able to give a right answer to the questions raised by the parable of the talents and by the parable of the sheep and the goats concerning its faith and love. The question is really about the oil. Will the virgins have a supply of oil for their lamps when they go out to meet the Bridegroom when he suddenly appears? If the lamps stand for the congregation's witness by word and deed, by its faith and love, then the oil represents the Holy Spirit, without which the congregation cannot believe, love, and hope. Does it know that the Spirit is absolutely indispensable for its existence in the interim period? Is it walking according to the Spirit and in the Spirit (Rom. 8:4; Gal. 5:16, 25)? Does it know that it can hope to participate in the marriage supper of the Lamb only if it lives by "the promise of the Spirit" (Gal. 3:14; Eph. 1:13)? The "promise of the Spirit" may be understood in two ways: the Spirit is promised, and the Spirit promises.[25]

1. Jesus has promised to give the Spirit. He is the Giver of the water of life. The congregation hopes in Jesus' promise of the Spirit, without which it cannot believe, love, and hope in Jesus, and without which its eating and drinking cannot be a Eucharist or an Agape or a Marriage Supper, and therefore cannot be in remembrance of Jesus. It is a confident hope. For if we, being evil, know how to give good gifts to our children, how much more will the heavenly Father give the Holy Spirit to those who ask him? If we ask, seek, and knock, it will be opened to us (Luke 11:9–13; Matt. 7:7–12).

The church believes that Jesus has kept his promise and that time and again throughout its history since Pentecost it has received the Spirit. But it knows that it has had the Spirit only as the "poor in spirit" who hunger and thirst. The church never comes to possess, control, or dispose of the Spirit. It cannot dispense the Spirit. The Spirit is free: it blows when and where it wills. As the congregation gathers around the table, it fervently prays: "Come, Holy Spirit." It goes from one meal to the next in anticipation of the Spirit.

2. The Spirit promises. He does not come empty-handed. What the Spirit promises is the manifestation and knowledge

of the crucified and risen Lord, of the reconciliation and redemption of the world, of the Lord in whom God's name is
hallowed, his kingdom has come and will come, his will has
been done and will be done on earth as it is in heaven. The
Spirit promises Jesus. "He who has an ear, let him hear what
the Spirit says to the churches," that Jesus is coming soon
(Rev. 3:13, 11). Jesus was not deluded about his imminent
return, and the Spirit does not delude or disappoint those
who wait for him. Jesus' coming is not delayed or postponed;
he is at hand. "Behold, I stand at the door and knock; if any
one hears my voice and opens the door, I will come in to him
and eat with him, and he with me." (Rev. 3:20.) If the
servants of the Master are awake and waiting for him, and
open to him at once when he comes and knocks, he will "have
them sit at table, and he will come and serve them" (Luke
12:35-40). This is the hope in which the congregation assembles: that the same Jesus who suffered, died, and rose
again will come through closed doors and will stand among
them and say to them: "Peace be with you" (John 20:19).
Paul can go so far as to say that "the Lord is the Spirit," that
is, the mode of Christ's presence by which he manifests himself to us is the Spirit. "And where the Spirit of the Lord is,
there is freedom"—freedom to behold the glory of the Lord
and, in beholding his glory, to be "changed into his likeness";
that is, to begin to believe, love, and hope in the likeness of
Jesus' trust, love, and hope in his heavenly Father.

As Jesus comes again as the Giver of the water of life, so
he comes as the Giver of food and drink. As the congregation
gives thanks for Jesus in whom and through whom it has
been given all food and drink, so it prays that through Jesus
Christ it will receive its daily bread. It hopes in the coming
of Jesus as the Host who furnishes his Table, nay more, that
he will come as the true *diakonos*, the unseen waiter who will
serve them. In reality, eating and drinking is an act of hope
when it is the prayer: "Give us this day our daily bread."

When the congregation puts its trust and confidence in Jesus it is not deceived or disappointed. It is not despondent, disheartened, or despairing. It is not anxious or worried about the morrow. Unlike Gentile unbelievers, who do not know that Jesus is coming soon, the congregation does not fretfully ask: "What shall we eat? Or what shall we drink? Or what shall we wear"?

We are thinking of the passages in Matt. 6:25–34 and Luke 12:22–31. It is important to consider the context in which Jesus uttered these words. In Luke's Gospel they are immediately preceded by the parable of the rich landowner who was never satisfied, and whose business had so expanded that he had to pull down his barns and build bigger ones in which to store his grain and possessions. In Matthew's Gospel they are preceded by the warning not to lay up treasures on earth where moth and rust consume and thieves break in and steal, and by the assertion that it is impossible to serve God and Mammon. In each case Jesus says: "Therefore," that is, because you are so rich, "do not be anxious." Jesus points out that the tendency to anxiety lies not so much with the poor as with the rich who have made doubly and triply sure that they have security in order to be free of financial worries.[26] Anxiety increases as riches increase. This truth applies not only to individuals but to nations and to the great power blocs in East and West. The greater the power, the greater the anxiety and fear. And anxiety dictates that the high standard of living attained must be maintained at all costs and by any means, even by atomic bombs. This is the reason why our Western world, especially the United States, has been obsessed by fear and anxiety. It is because we are the rich landowner among the underprivileged peoples of the world, because we have laid up enormous fortunes on earth where thieves—the Communists—could break in and steal. The tyranny of anxiety is broken only where Jesus is known as the Lord and men hope in the coming of his kingdom and righteousness. Then all those things for which Gentile unbelievers seek—food, drink, and clothing—shall be added unto them. For "your heavenly Father knows that you need them all."

Those who hope in the coming of Jesus do not need to lay up treasures on earth nor do they need to hoard their daily bread, as the children of Israel hoarded the manna in the wilderness. Nor will they waste their substance in riotous living. Still less will they resort to violence in order to protect or to increase their possessions. They will not behave as did that wicked servant who said to himself, "My master is delayed," and who began to beat up his fellow servants, and to eat and drink with the drunken (Matt. 24:48 f.). Where there is no hope there is no love. Inhumanity and violence in the world are in proportion to its hopelessness. Yet the world may hear: "Behold, the judge is standing at the doors" (James 5:9). The Master is coming, at an hour when he is not expected, to establish a measure of justice, freedom, and peace. He will punish the wicked servants and succor the oppressed. (Cf. James 5:1-11.) Luke adds the thought that the punishment will be more severe for a church which knew about the "Master's will" but neither proclaimed the hope of his coming nor lived according to it (Luke 12:45 ff.).

The prayer for daily bread is a prayer for food for the physical body, and it includes a prayer that Jesus will come bringing a little justice, freedom, and peace for our as yet unredeemed world. It includes a prayer for rulers and all those in authority who are also Christ's ministers. A spiritualizing of the meaning of bread is to be rejected, as though Jesus were not concerned about the things of the body, as if he does not hasten to come to right the wrongs in society, or as if it were unworthy of his followers to be concerned about food and drink and about those who are exploited and oppressed. Yet modern scholarship is surely right when it declares that the fourth petition of the Lord's Prayer is at one and the same time a prayer for earthly bread to meet the hunger and need of the present day and also for the future bread in the eschatological kingdom.[27] That bread is the bread of eternal life, of which earthly bread is but a sign. That bread is received by faith even now in the "last times" between the kingdom that has come in Christ's resurrection and its final manifestation. The prayer for bread for the morrow is therefore a prayer that Jesus will one day come in such a way that we will be able to *see* what now we can only *believe*, namely, that he is the Bread of eternal life. He who hopes in the coming of Jesus is not anxious about his impending death. Did not Jesus say, "Which of you by being anxious can add one cubit to his span of life?" It is folly for an individual or for a people to worry about how long they are going to live. No matter how much one frets, life will not be prolonged one day. As Martin Luther King once said, it is not a matter of how long we live, but how we have lived; that is, whether in the span of life allotted to us we have sought first the kingdom and its righteousness in all our private and public affairs. The fear of death is removed from us in faith and hope in Christ who has come and comes again as the bread of eternal life.

What we have been trying to say is that all our personal and collective hopes as individuals, as a church, as various social groups, as a nation, indeed, as a family of nations, are embraced in the hope of the coming of Jesus. All penultimate and ultimate hopes are in Jesus. He is our hope, the hope of Israel and the hope of the world. The ultimate hope, upon which all penultimate hopes are grounded, is, of course, that one day Jesus will come in such a way that the tremendous transformation of all things that has occurred in his death and has been revealed only in his resurrection will be manifested in the life of *all* men and *all* creation. As the congregation eats and drinks in hope, it is conscious of the tension between the "already" and the "not yet." It has been "born anew to a living hope through the resurrection of Jesus Christ from the dead" (I Peter 1:3). But it is conscious of the contradiction between hope and sight, between what we are in Christ and what we are in ourselves. "It does not yet appear what we shall be, but we know that when he appears we shall be like him" (I John 3:2). Now our life "is hid with Christ in God. When Christ who is our life appears, then [we] also will appear with him in glory" (Col. 3:3 f.).

Apart from inklings of it in little deeds of faith, love, and hope, the great transformation is almost completely invisible in the world. Mankind—Christians included—continues to sin, suffer, and die. There are still wars and rumors of wars, earthquakes, famine, and pestilence. Jesus has overcome the world, but in the world we still have tribulation (John 16:33). What oppresses us and all men is not the lack or absence of the power of the resurrection of Jesus but the fact that this power is not evident and therefore is apparently absent, and the fact that the reconciliation and redemption of the world can be observed and experienced only in the living Jesus Christ himself (Barth). The good news of the triumphant death of Jesus is proclaimed despite the contradiction of all empirical evidence.

Thus the congregation is well aware that the Lord's Supper is but a foretaste and pledge of the marriage feast of the Lamb on a new earth and under a new heaven in which righteousness dwells. It hopes for the fulfillment of Jesus' promise: "I will raise him up at the last day" (John 6:39, 40, 44, 54). Then we will *see* and *be* what now we only *believe*, namely, that Jesus is the food of eternal life and that we have already passed from death unto life. But when we try to describe the marriage feast at the final parousia we stutter and stammer in the brokenness of our thoughts, words, and deeds. How can we, who live in the middle, speak about the Beginning and the End, the Alpha and the Omega, except in the language of fantasy and myth? It is no accident that the opening chapters of Genesis and the entire book of Revelation are cast in the most mythical language of the Bible. Not that the creation and the consummation are unhistorical; they are the pure acts of God which the church has stammeringly confessed to be *creatio ex nihilo*. Freely acknowledging that we need not less but more mythology, we can do no better than to avail ourselves of the language of the last chapters of the Bible.

According to the witness of John, the marriage supper in its final form will take place in "the holy city, new Jerusalem, coming down out of heaven from God, prepared as a bride adorned for her husband" (Rev. 21:2). It will be a city in which the power of evil, which threatened the first creation, will be no more. The sea will be no more. Moreover, "nothing unclean shall enter it, nor anyone who practices abomination or falsehood" (Rev. 21:27; cf. chs. 20:10, 14; 21:8; 22:18). The contradiction of sin, suffering, and death will be unequivocally removed: "Death shall be no more, neither shall there be mourning nor crying nor pain any more, for the former things have passed away" (Rev. 21:4). The city will "have no need of sun or moon to shine upon it, for the glory of God is its light, and its lamp is the Lamb" (Rev. 21:23; cf. chs. 21:25; 22:5). There will be no succession of day and night, no recurring seedtime and harvest, no slaughter of animals, no economic and military struggle for food. Then the only food will be the fruit of "the tree of life" which is the Lamb, and the only drink will be of "the river of the water of life, bright as crystal, flowing from the throne of God and the Lamb" (Rev. 22:1 f.)—the Spirit of the Father and the Son.[28] Indeed, in the city there will be no temple, "for its temple is the Lord God the Almighty and the Lamb" (Rev. 21:22). There will be no need for eating and drinking in remembrance of Jesus, no need to proclaim his death by word and deed, no need for faith and repentance. For the servants of the Lamb "shall worship him; they shall see his face"

(Rev. 22:3 f.). Meanwhile, being strangers, exiles, and pilgrims on earth, we "see through a glass darkly." Hence we look "forward to the city which has foundations, whose builder and maker is God" (Heb. 11:10, 13–16; 13:14; I Peter 2:11).

We have concluded our ethical and Biblical inquiry. We have sought an answer to three questions: Why, what, and how may and must men eat and drink with Jesus? We now summarize the answer we have received. Jesus Christ is the Giver of food and drink, the Bread of life, and the Giver of the water of life. In him the commandment to eat and drink has been fulfilled. He has come and will come again to be present with all men, and his preserving, reconciling, and saving presence is revealed to his congregation through the Holy Spirit. Therefore the Lord's Supper, as Eucharist, Agape, and Marriage Supper, is a sign and proclamation that all men may and must eat and drink with Jesus in faith, love, and hope.

Appendix I.

WHETHER JESUS IS
EATEN IN THE LORD'S SUPPER

In his essay on "The Meaning of the Lord's Supper in Primitive Christianity," [1] Oscar Cullmann, following Hans Lietzmann,[2] has shown that the earliest Christian liturgies have no reference to eating Jesus in the Lord's Supper. The ancient Egyptian liturgy, of which the model may be found in Serapion,[3] and which may be traced back to the Didache or "Teaching of the Twelve Apostles," and so to the most ancient Christian liturgy we possess, has no reference to the so-called words of institution, or to the body and blood of Christ, but only to "the Holy Vine of David thy servant." The prayers refer to the return of the Lord and to the fellowship of those assembled for the meal. The notion that the Eucharist is a means of grace is also absent from the Didache.[4] In complete contrast is the liturgy of St. Hippolytus, which is "dominated by the idea of *the death of Christ* and is above all inspired by the Words of Institution as these are found in St. Paul and in the Synoptists." [5] If the date of the "Apostolic Tradition" was within a year or two either way of A.D. 215, as Gregory Dix believes, then from that date we have the earliest sacramental liturgy of the Eucharist.

The sacramental understanding of the Eucharist begins earlier, with Ignatius of Antioch (d. about 117). For him it is a means of union with Christ, and it is a true participation in the blessings of Christ. He speaks of breaking "one Bread which is the medicine of immortality and the antidote against death enabling us to live forever in Jesus Christ." [6] "If any one is not inside the sanctuary, he lacks God's bread." [7] "Be careful, then, to observe a single Eucharist. For there is one flesh of our Lord, Jesus Christ, and one cup of his blood that makes us one, and one altar, just as there is one bishop along with the presbytery and the deacons." [8] The reference to the "altar" is the first suggestion that the Eucharist is a sacrifice. "They [the Docetists] hold aloof from the Eucharist and from services of prayer, because they refuse to admit that the Eucharist is the flesh of our Saviour Jesus Christ, which suffered for our sins and which, in his goodness, the Father raised." [9] From these passages it is evident that for Ignatius the Eucharist was a cultic meal in which the flesh of Christ is present and eaten, and which, as such, is a means of union with Christ and of participation in the fruits of his death and resurrection. Moreover, in Ignatius we find the first application of "mysteries" to the Eucharist: "Those too who are deacons of Jesus Christ's 'mysteries' must give complete satisfaction to everyone. For they do not serve mere food and drink but minister to God's Church." [10]

In his First Apology, written about A.D. 155, Justin Martyr gives an account of the Eucharist. [11] We quote in full Sec. 66, in which Justin gives his understanding of the meaning of the rite:

> This food we call Eucharist, of which no one is allowed to partake except one who believes that the things we teach are true, and has received the washing for forgiveness of sins and for rebirth, and who lives as Christ handed down to us. For we do not receive these things as common bread or common drink; but as Jesus Christ our Saviour being incarnate by God's word took flesh and blood for our salvation, so also we have been taught that the food consecrated by the word of prayer which comes from him, from which our flesh and blood are nourished by transformation, is the flesh and blood of that incarnate Jesus. For the apostles in the memoirs composed by them, which are called Gospels, thus handed down what was commanded them: that Jesus, taking bread and having given thanks, said, "Do this for my memorial, this is my body"; and likewise taking the cup and giving thanks he said, "This is my

blood"; and gave it to them alone. This also the wicked demons in imitation handed down as something to be done in the mysteries of Mithra; for bread and a cup of water are brought out in their secret rites of initiation, with certain invocations which you either know or can learn.

Certain points are to be noted:

1. The conditions for partaking of the Eucharist are not faith in and love for Christ but (*a*) belief "that the things we teach are true"; (*b*) baptism; and (*c*) living according to principles handed down to us by Christ.

2. A distinction is made between common bread and drink and, by implication, the holy, sacramental bread and drink. No such distinction is found in the New Testament; on the contrary, "nothing is unclean of itself."

3. An analogy is drawn "between the assumption of flesh and blood by Jesus Christ in the Incarnation and the consecration of bread and wine, which possess the ordinary properties of nutrition (*kata metabolēn* refers to the assimilation of the food by digestion), so that they become the flesh and blood of Christ." [12]

4. The incarnation occurs "through the word of God"; ordinary bread and drink become "the flesh and blood of that incarnate Jesus" through being "consecrated [literally "eucharistized," that is, blessed by the prayer of thanksgiving] by the word of prayer which comes from him." The reference is undoubtedly to Jesus' taking bread and the cup and giving thanks and blessing it at the Last Supper, though some scholars hold that it refers to his words, "This is my body; this is my blood." In either case Justin evidently believed that Jesus' words were not just a proclamation and a thanksgiving but that by the repetition of his words a miraculous change was effected whereby ordinary food and drink became the flesh and blood of the Jesus who was made flesh. Whereas in the Didache the Eucharist is a "thank offering" and consists of a service of prayer and praise in which the blessings of creation and redemption are commemorated, the term "Eucharist" is here applied to the consecrated food which is identified with the flesh and blood of Jesus.

5. Authority for the repetition of this act of consecration is said to come from the apostles in their Gospels who thus handed

down what was commanded them, "Do this in remembrance of me." The Lucan and Pauline command to eat and drink in remembrance of Jesus Christ, that is, of what he did in his incarnation, death, and resurrection, is changed to mean a command to change bread and drink into the body and blood of Christ by the word of thanksgiving.

6. Finally, Justin recognizes an "imitation" between (a) the command of Jesus and that of the "wicked demons"; (b) between the handing down ("the tradition") of the apostles in the Gospels and the handing down of something to be done in the mysteries of Mithra, and (c) between the Eucharist and the bread and cup of water in the secret rites of initiation of Mithra. Apparently for Justin a significant difference between the Christian and the pagan rites is the fact that Jesus gave the command to "do this in remembrance of me" to the apostles alone. When he states that the mysteries of Mithra were done in imitation of the Christian Eucharist, the suggestion is that the Eucharist was historically prior to the mysteries.

From the time of Ignatius and Justin Martyr there has persisted down to the present a belief in the *mysterium* or *sacramentum* of repeatedly eating and drinking Christ's body and blood. The belief has been held by the main branches of Christendom— Eastern Orthodox, Roman Catholic, Lutheran, Reformed, and Episcopalian. Although there has been considerable disagreement as to *how* Christ is present in the Lord's Supper and *how* he is eaten, whether more realistically or more symbolically and spiritually, all have been in agreement that Christ is present and is somehow eaten. It will not be our task here to trace the development of the doctrine in the first five centuries through Irenaeus, Tertullian, and Cyprian, in the Alexandrian school of Origen and Clement, through the realistic conception of the Eucharist in the Eastern church fathers which passed to the West through Ambrose who, significantly, entitled one of his treatises *The Mysteries*.

It has been contended that Augustine presented a figurative or symbolic view of the sacraments "which delayed for some centuries the complete acceptance in the West of the Ambrosian view." This contention is based to a large extent upon Augustine's famous definition of a sacrament as "visible signs of divine things," [13] and upon the distinction he made between the *sacramentum* (the outward part) and the *res* (the inward part) and between the sacrament and the "virtue" of the sacrament.[14] There is also his statement that "the word is added to the element and it becomes a sacrament, as if it itself [were] also a visible word." [15] It is true that Augustine could speak of Christ delivering to the disciples the "figure" (*figuram*) or "sign" (*signum*) of his body and blood,[16] and could maintain that the sign must be carefully distinguished from that which it signifies: "It is not that which is seen that feeds, but that which is believed." [17] "Believe, and you have eaten." [18] On the other hand, it would be a mistake to think that for Augustine the sacraments were bare signs. Although he strongly emphasized the necessity of faith and the spirituality of the gift, he certainly held to a spiritual presence of Christ in the sacraments and to a spiritual eating and drinking of his body and blood. Indeed, in places he gives a realistic interpretation. In his *Enarrations on the Twenty-third Psalm* he wrote: "Christ was carried in his hands, when in giving His own body, he said, 'This is my body.' For he carried that body in his hands." [19] "When he gave his own body and his own blood, he took in his hands what the faithful know; and in a certain manner he carried himself, when he said, 'This is my body.' " [20] Elsewhere we read: "Not all bread, but that bread which receives the blessing of Christ, becomes the body of Christ." [21] As if anticipating the debate between the Lutherans and the Reformed, Augustine appears to side with the former when he insists that "the identification of the elements with the body and blood of Christ is so complete that even the wicked recipients of the Sacrament receive Christ's body and blood as really, though with different effects, as those who partake of the Sacrament worthily." [22] Thus in his book against the Donatists, *On Baptism*, he says that "it is the body and blood of the Lord no less in the case of those of whom the Apostle said, 'Who eats unworthily eats and drinks judgment to himself.' " [23] Similarly in one of his sermons he states that there are two ways of "eating that flesh and drinking that blood," one of which leads to the recipient abiding in Christ and Christ in him, the other of which leads to judgment.[24]

Whether one attributes to Augustine a symbolical or realistic interpretation of the Eucharist, or a combination of both, his great contribution lay in clarifying the church's sacramental understanding of itself and of baptism and the Lord's Supper as it developed in the first four centuries, and of offering an analysis which became authoritative for Western Christendom down to the present. Although Roman Catholic, Lutheran, and Reformed churchmen could disagree about the *mode* of Christ's presence in the elements, all could agree with Augustine's definition of the sacrament as a visible sign of an invisible grace. All could agree that Christ's body and blood are somehow given in the sacrament and that somehow they are eaten and drunk. All could agree with Augustine's uses of the words *consecratio*, *benedictio*, and *sanctificare* to denote that act of consecration by which the elements of bread and wine become a sacrament and a means of grace.[25] But there was one outstanding exception: Huldreich Zwingli!

Alone among the Reformers, and like a voice crying in the wilderness, Zwingli raised his voice against the answer which, since Ignatius and Justin Martyr, had been given to the question whether Jesus is eaten in the Lord's Supper. Alone among the Reformers he took the trouble to investigate the meaning of the word "sacrament." Alone among the Reformers he saw clearly that a sacrament is not a means of grace.[26] Zwingli deserves a better hearing than he has had.

For Zwingli the one means of grace was the once-and-for-all sacrifice of Christ to be believed through the power of the Holy Spirit. It was a position which he consistently maintained in all his writings from the adoption of his *Sixty-seven Articles* at the First Zurich Disputation in January, 1523, until he composed *A Short and Clear Exposition of the Christian Faith* shortly before his death on October 11, 1531. It is spelled out in some detail in his *Commentary on True and False Religion*, published in March, 1525. Zwingli found three meanings of the word "sacrament." (1) "Sacrament" is a pledge which litigants deposited at some altar, and the winner later got back his pledge or money. (2) "Sacrament" is an oath. (3) There is a "military sacrament," by which soldiers are bound to obey their general. Zwingli recognized that the Latin translation of the New Testament has *sacramentum* for mystery. But he explained that "the word does not express that, nor do I know any Latin word which really gives the meaning of *mystērion*, because *arcanum* ("secret") has a wider application than *mystērion*, and *sacrum* ("sacred") is of a somewhat narrower scope." [27] Although Zwingli did not seem to know that "sacrament" came to have the meaning of *mystērion*, derived not from the New Testament but from the Hellenistic Mystery religions, that is, the re-presentation of the cultic deity and a means of grace, he did see that "a sacrament is nothing else than an initiatory ceremony of pledging. . . . When this has been accomplished, the person initiated is bound to perform for the office, order, or institution to which he has devoted himself what the institution or office demands. A sacrament, therefore, since it cannot be anything more than an initiation or public inauguration, cannot have any power to free the conscience. That can be freed by God alone." [28] Nor can the sacraments have any cleansing power.[29] They do not create or strengthen faith.[30] Faith does not occur when they are performed, for the Holy Spirit, by which faith is quickened, can be given before or after baptism.[31] "The sacraments are, then, signs or ceremonies . . . by which a man proves to the Church that he either aims to be, or is, a soldier of Christ, and which inform the whole Church rather than yourself of your faith. For if your faith is not so perfect as not to need a ceremonial sign to confirm it, it is not faith. For faith is that by which we rely on the mercy of God unwaveringly, firmly, and singleheartedly." [32]

In his treatise *Of Baptism*, published on May 27, 1525, Zwingli wrote: "In our native tongue [that is, in common usage] the word ["sacrament"] suggests something that has power to take away sin and to make us holy. But this is a serious perversion. For only Jesus Christ and no external thing can take away the sins of us Christians and make us holy. . . . The word sacrament means a covenant sign or pledge. . . . The man who receives the mark of baptism is the one who is resolved to hear what God says to him, to learn the divine precepts and to live his life in accordance with them. And the man who in the remembrance or Supper gives thanks to God in the congregation testifies to the fact that from the very heart he rejoices in the death of Christ and thanks him for it." [33] In "An Account of the Faith of Huldreich Zwingli sub-

mitted to the German Emperor Charles V at the Diet of Augsburg" (July 3, 1530) he reiterated his stand. "I believe, indeed
I know, that all the sacraments are so far from conferring grace
that they do not even convey or dispense it. . . . For as grace
comes from or is given by the Divine Spirit . . . so this gift per-
tains to the Spirit alone. Moreover, a channel or vehicle is not
necessary to the Spirit." [34] "If he [a man] is prepared by the Spirit
for the reception of grace, I ask whether this be done through the
sacraments as a channel or independent of the sacraments? If the
sacraments mediate, man is prepared by the sacrament for the
sacrament, and thus there will be a process *ad infinitum*; for sacrament will be required as a preparation for a sacrament. If we be
prepared without the sacrament for the reception of sacramental
grace, the Spirit is present in his goodness before the sacrament,
and hence grace has been shown and is present before the sacrament is administered. From this it follows . . . that the sacraments are given as public testimony of that grace which is previously present to every individual." [35]

After Zwingli had submitted to the emperor the account of his
faith, John Eck, who defended the Roman Catholic position at
the Diet of Augsburg, wrote a "Refutation of the Articles of
Zwingli." [36] To this Zwingli published a "Letter of Huldreich
Zwingli to the Most Illustrious Princes of Germany Assembled at
Augsburg, Regarding the Insults of Eck," August 27, 1530. In this
particular work we detect a slight shift in Zwingli's thinking. Dis-
cussing the doctrine of the early church fathers he asserted: "I
have never denied that Christ's body is present in the Supper
sacramentally and mysteriously." [37] However, he immediately explains that "it belongs to faith that the things are or become
present, and not to the sacraments. . . . Hence it is apparent
that the sacraments cannot justify nor give grace, for we know no
other justification than that of faith." [38] "That which is symbolized by the sacraments is at hand before we use the sacraments.
. . . The sacraments simply make confession of, bear witness to,
and call into use what we have before." [39] Yet Zwingli could talk
about bread, being blessed by the word and prayer, being converted into Christ's "sacramental body." [40] He could grant that
Christ's body is eaten "mysteriously" or "sacramentally" but not

"physically." "My opponents say the material and substantial body is offered, I say the sacramental. . . . Did Christ offer his body to be eaten materially and physically or spiritually? If they say 'spiritually,' they withdraw from their opinion and come over to mine." [41] "I have long been saying that the body of Christ is in the Supper to the eye of faith" [42]—which, in fact, Zwingli had not been saying in all of his previous writings. "Thus, I say, do I understand the highly figurative and hyperbolic language regarding the Eucharist. And, as I have often borne witness, I can easily put up with all expressions of this kind, provided we do not go on to understand physically the thing said of spiritual partaking." [43]

Zwingli's meaning here is not entirely clear. Did he mean that as we eat and drink bread and wine we spiritually eat and drink the body and blood of Christ? Or did he mean that as we eat and drink bread and wine we do so as a testimony to a spiritual eating and drinking that is faith that Christ has been slain for us? In the light of all that he had written we must assume the latter. Moreover, in his A *Short and Clear Exposition of the Christian Faith* (written in July, 1531—he met his death on October 11—and published by Bullinger in February, 1536), Zwingli clarified what he meant by sacramental eating. "If I may put it more precisely, to eat the body of Christ sacramentally is to eat the body of Christ with the heart and the mind in conjunction with the sacrament." [44] "The sacraments do give faith, but only historical faith (an acceptance of the historical truth of the events proclaimed). All celebrations, monuments and statues give historical faith, that is, they remind us of some event, refreshing the memory like the feast of the passover amongst the Hebrews or the remission of debts at Athens or it may be they commemorate some victory like the stone at Ebenezer. . . . But only to the faithful and pious does it [the Lord's Supper] testify that Christ suffered for us. For it is only those who have been taught inwardly by the Spirit to know the mystery of the divine goodness who can know and confess that Christ suffered for us: it is they alone who receive Christ. For no one comes to Christ except the Father draw him. . . . It is quite impossible that the Supper should give faith: for faith must be present before we come." [45] We conclude, therefore, that Zwingli, alone among the Reformers, saw clearly that a sacrament is not a means of grace or even of faith; it is an ethical response to God's one justifying and saving work in the death of Christ and to the outpouring of the Holy Spirit.

This is not to deny that there are serious gaps and weaknesses in Zwingli's doctrine of the Eucharist. In his anxiety to prove that the body and blood of Christ are not eaten and drunk in the Eucharist he advanced a questionable Christology to the effect that the humanity of Jesus is in heaven at the right hand of God the Father and that He is present in his divinity inasmuch as God is present everywhere. The Lutherans rightly rejected Zwingli's separation of the two natures in Christ. Yet consistent with his basic definition of a sacrament Zwingli never advanced the theory that Christ in his divinity is present in, with, and under bread and wine, so that to this extent they would become holy or divine bread and wine and thus a means of saving grace. Zwingli failed to show that Jesus Christ in both his humanity and divinity is particularly present through the Spirit where two or three are gathered together in his name and generally present to all men. He did not make plain how Christians in particular and all men in general may eat and drink *with* Jesus.[46] Moreover, Zwingli failed to draw out the ethical implications of his own nonsacramental view of the Eucharist. He stressed that it is an act of thanksgiving and praise, but he did not show that it is also an act of love and of hope.

Yet in spite of these shortcomings he saw the crucial issue in a way that Calvin never did, namely, that the once-and-for-all sacrifice of Christ is the one means of saving grace, and that therefore the sacraments cannot even be a cognitive or spiritual means of grace. Indeed, Calvin's much lauded effort to find a *via media* between the Lutheran and Zwinglian positions only served to becloud the central issue and had the effect of postponing the recovery of an ethical interpretation of the Lord's Supper. We concur with Karl Barth's observation: "When we read what the *Confess. Helv. Post.* [published thirty-five years after Zwingli's death] has to say about the sacraments in general and baptism in particular, we should never suspect, if we did not already know, that its author Heinrich Bullinger was Zwingli's immediate successor. This work is wholly influenced by the dominant Reformed tradition of Calvin, so much so that in the doctrine of the Lord's Supper there is even a strange attempt at assimilation to the Roman Catholic doctrine of a change in the elements." [47]

But how is one to account for the triumph of sacramentalism in the early and medieval church which, in spite of Zwingli's protest, was not overcome at the Reformation? A plausible explanation of the rise of sacramentalism was offered by the *religionsgeschichtliche Schule* or the study of comparative religions in the first quarter of the present century. This school made an intensive study of the Greek Mystery cults and drew comparisons between them and Christianity. It was hoped that by discovering the relationships between the Christian and pagan mysteries it would be possible to establish the contribution made by the Mystery cults to the genesis of Christianity, or at least to its development in the first centuries of the church. At first Richard Reitzenstein, a leading exponent of the school, held that the Iranian redemption mystery provided the original source material of Christian doctrine. Later he contended that the source is to be found in the supposedly pre-Christian cult of the Mandaeans.[48] Hugo Rahner has observed that Wilhelm Bousset, in the second edition of his work *Kyrios Christos* (1921),[49] argued that "all the mystery cults of later antiquity . . . had one feature in common. In their mystical and liturgical action they sought to imitate the dying and rising cult god and so partake in the power he could effectively exercise in the next world, and this was also the fundamental character of the Christian doctrine of sacrament and redemption." [50] Bousset saw in the cultic imitation of the dying and rising god that is common to all the mysteries "the spiritual atmosphere that surrounds Paul's dying and rising in Christ." In Rahner's judgment, Alfred Loisy was even more radical. For Loisy "the 'myth' of Christianity is the great drama of world redemption through Christ, which Paul, under the influence of the god-man myths of his time, read into the simple Gospel story of Jesus. The 'rite' of Christianity, however, is the smaller drama of the mystical initiation of the individual." [51]

Understandably there were scholars who were opposed to the radical thesis of those who claimed that there is a genetic relationship or one of historical causality between the Hellenistic Mystery

religions and Christianity in general and the Christian sacraments
in particular. F. Cumont[52] and C. Clemen,[53] as well as others,
warned against equating the Hellenistic mysteries with the Christian sacraments or deriving the sacraments from the mysteries.
Rahner refers to the work done by the monks of Maria Laach
under the leadership of Dom Odo Casel on the so-called "Mystery
doctrine" (Mysterienlehre). While unequivocally rejecting all
theories of genetic derivation, it saw "a kind of common ground
of the 'cult eidos' of the mystery which served as a kind of imperfect and shadowy prefiguration of the reality which was brought
by God to its final fulfilment in the mystery of Christ. This eidos
. . . is the 'cultic presence of the redemptive act' constantly
renewed in mystery. Each time the mystic rite is accomplished,
the redeeming action of God dead and risen again is ever effectively renewed for the worshiping community, independently of
any consideration of time and space." [54] Still other scholars took
the position that although there are analogies and parallels between the Mystery religions and their rites on the one hand, and
Christianity and its sacraments on the other, and although Christianity may have adopted the thought forms of the Mystery
religions in order to make the unique event of the death and resurrection of Jesus Christ understandable, they differ essentially in
content. F. Lang,[55] for example, argues that the main difference
between Christianity and the Mystery religions consists in the fact
that the gods of the Mystery religions are mythical figures which
in the last analysis represent a timeless, natural process, while the
apostles proclaim a once-and-for-all historical person as the Lord
and Redeemer whom God has raised from the dead. Moreover, in
the Mystery religions it is not a matter of the forgiveness of sins
and resurrection in the Biblical sense, but primarily of participation in immortality. In the Mystery religions the new life is
mediated through a sacramental act of deification, whereas the
New Testament emphasizes the moral realization of new life
through the obedience of faith.

There is no doubt that we have to think further in the direction Lang has indicated. At the outset it has to be seen that Jesus
Christ in his death and resurrection is not a myth or the person-
ification of a timeless myth. He is not the embodiment of the

principle of dying and rising again. He is the once-and-for-all event in history in which the fallen and mortal nature of men was assumed by the Son of God and radically transformed: justified, sanctified, and glorified. There is indeed an identification of human nature with the Son of God who dies on the cross and was raised from the dead. But this identification occurred once and for all in the hypostatic union—in the history of the birth, life, death, and resurrection of the Son of God as man. Moreover, it occurred once and for all times. That is to say, what occurred then is present and valid for all men now, inasmuch as Jesus Christ is the same yesterday, today, and tomorrow. It is the unique historicity of God's work of salvation in Jesus Christ which precludes the possibility of repeated identifications of men with Christ's dying and rising through cultric rites and sacraments.

Unfortunately, as we have shown above, the early church fathers lost sight of the unique historicity of the saving event in Jesus Christ and interpreted Baptism and the Lord's Supper analogously to the cultic rites of the Mystery religions. In marked contrast to the New Testament they explicitly referred to Baptism and the Lord's Supper as "mysteries" and the Latin fathers translated *mystērion* by *sacramentum*.

In the Gospels the term *mystērion* is used by Jesus only with reference to the purpose of the parables: "To you has been given the secret of the kingdom of God, but for those outside everything is in parables" (Mark 4:11; cf. Matt. 13:11; Luke 8:10). Parabolic teaching serves to conceal the mystery of the reign of God —a mystery disclosed to the disciples but not to others. The mystery has to do with the fact of the coming of the kingdom which is identical with Jesus himself as the Messiah. Likewise for Paul, Christ is the *mystērion* of God (Col. 1:27; 2:2; 4:3). He is the "secret and hidden wisdom of God . . . decreed before the ages for our glorification" (I Cor. 2:7) which the apostle proclaims (I Cor. 2:1). As G. Bornkamm observes, in the section in I Cor. 2:6–16 Paul is combating a mystery *gnōsis* with the *sophia* of God, which is the divine will to save fulfilled in the crucifixion of Jesus (I Cor. 1:24) and which is "a stumbling block to Jews and folly to Gentiles" (I Cor. 1:23). It is a wisdom which is hid from "the rulers of this age" and which "God has revealed to us through

the Spirit" (I Cor. 2:8, 10). According to the letter to the Ephesians the mystery of the will of God to unite all things in heaven
and on earth in Christ is set forth in Christ as a plan (Eph. 1:9 f.)
—which plan is "the plan of the mystery hidden for ages in God
who created all things" (Eph. 3:9), "the mystery hidden for
ages and generations but now made manifest to his saints" (Col.
1:26). According to Eph. 3:4 ff., the mystery of Christ is *revealed*
and *made known* to the prophets and apostles and consists in the
fact that Gentiles are made fellow heirs with the Jews, and members of one body through the cross (cf. Eph. 2:11–22; Rom., chs.
9 to 11). And according to Eph. 5:21–33 the mystery that is
prefigured in Gen. 2:24 is the relation of Christ and his church.

Elsewhere in the New Testament mention is made of the
mysterium iniquitatis (II Thess. 2:7; Rev. 17:5, 7). These are
anti-God and anti-Christian powers. But their mystery is to be
seen strictly in relation to and in subordination to the power of
God. The mystery of lawlessness is at work now but it is restrained
by Christ, who will reveal it and destroy it at his appearing. The
mystery of the harlot Babylon is revealed by God to "his servant
John" by an angel and "the Lamb will conquer, for he is Lord of
lords and King of kings." The mystery of iniquity is its subjection
to Christ and its provisional and transitory existence.

Never in the New Testament is *mystērion* used in connection
with Baptism and the Lord's Supper. Never is it used in reference
to a secret discipline. Never is there any warning against profaning the mysteries. Never is it used in connection with a supposed
consecration or blessing of water, bread, or wine.

Günther Bornkamm sums up the teaching of the New Testament as follows:

> In sum, μυστήριον is a rare expression in the N.T. which betrays
> no relation to the mystery cults. Where there seem to be con-
> nections (e.g. in sacramental passages), the term is not used;
> where it is used there are no such connections. In spite of certain
> analogies, there are thus serious objections against bringing Jesus
> or Paul under the category of The Mystagogue.[56]

Karl Barth puts the matter more pointedly:

One thing is clear: the New Testament speaks of "mystery" in the singular or in the plural exclusively with reference to God's action and revealing in history, but *not* with reference to human reactions corresponding to it. The πίστις, of whose mystery I Tim. 3:9 speaks, is obviously the *fides quae* and not the *fides qua creditur*, and the case is similar with the μυστήριον τῆς εὐσεβείας in I Tim. 3:16. Faith as a human work is never called a "mystery," nor the obedience of Christians, their love, their hope, etc. Nor are the existence and function of the ἐκκλησία, its proclamation of the Gospel or of its tradition as such. Nor are Baptism and the Lord's Supper so called.[57]

We have already seen that in the early church, *mystērion* became a fixed term for the sacraments. Although Justin Martyr and Tertullian inveigh against the pagan mysteries as devilish imitations of the Christian sacraments, it is clear that the same basic idea is seen in both, even if the content is different. "As the pagan mysteries actualize the destinies and acts of their gods in sacred actions, and thus give participants a share in them, so in the symbolical ritual of the Christian sacraments (always having the sense of a *signum efficax*) there takes place a cultic repetition and re-presentation of the historically unrepeatable redeeming act of Christ" (Bornkamm). By cultic celebration of the mysteries believers are taken up into the event of redemption and where Christ carries out the sacramental action Christ is present.

In the Latin Bible, *mystērion* was translated by *sacramentum*. Since *sacramentum* originally referred to a soldier's oath, the question has arisen how it could become a translation of *mystērion*. Bornkamm explains that the possibility is created by both the Latin and the Greek terms. Taking an oath has originally the character of an initiation and has an *occultum sacrum*. On the other hand, the mystery rites of initiation often entailed an oath. At any rate, "in Christian theological language 'sacrament' invariably acquired—not from the New Testament but from the language of Greek, Hellenistic mystery religion—the meaning of *mystērion*, that is, the representation of a cultic deity and a means of grace" (Barth).

Even if the New Testament nowhere speaks of the Lord's Supper as a sacrament or mystery, are there not exegetical grounds for believing that Jesus is somehow eaten and that the Supper is a means of grace and faith? In seeking an answer to this question we should note first of all that in the accounts of the post-Easter meals which Jesus took with his disciples in Luke 24:28–35, 36–43; John 21:9–15; and Acts 10:40–42, there is not so much as a hint that Jesus is eaten and his blood drunk. Nor is there any indication whatever that Jesus himself is eaten in the meals he took with his disciples, with the Pharisees, publicans, and tax collectors, and with Mary and Martha, and in the feedings of the multitudes before his death. In John's Gospel the changing of the water into wine at the wedding at Cana and the feeding of the multitude are called "signs" (John 2:11; 6:14, 26). But there is no suggestion that Jesus is eaten and his blood drunk in or with the signs. If, as scholars maintain, the Synoptic Gospels, and especially John, were written after Jesus' resurrection to give a theological interpretation of his person and work, it is surprising that they did not give *this* sacramental interpretation of the meals Jesus took with men before and after his resurrection. The evidence for a sacramental eating of Jesus in the New Testament is admittedly very meager. Lietzmann, Cullmann, and others freely concede that the predominant witness of the primitive church is to an eating and drinking "with Jesus." But they hold that another "type of Eucharist," in which Jesus is eaten, may be attributed to Paul and to the Synoptic accounts of the Last (Passover) Supper.

As far as Paul is concerned, it should be observed that the apostle does not give a thematic presentation of the Lord's Supper. He deals with it in passing as he corrects an abuse that had arisen in the Corinthian congregation. He deals with it in connection with ethical teachings and injunctions. Paul is concerned with the order or orderings of the assemblies of the congregation in a long section of his first epistle to the Corinthians—I Cor. 11:2 to 14:40. He deals with an improper eating and drinking of the bread and cup of the Lord (I Cor. 11:17–34) in the midst of instructions concerning the veiling of women in assemblies (ch. 11:2–16), the diversity of gifts and ministries of the one Spirit (ch. 12), love, without which all gifts and ministries are worthless (ch. 13), and the place of prophecy and speaking in tongues in the church gathering (ch. 14). The purpose and the conclusion of the whole section is that "all things should be done decently and in order" (ch. 14:40), "for God is not a God of confusion but of peace" (ch. 14:33). It is a matter, therefore, of the ethical response of the congregation, of its public service of Jesus Christ. The entire first fourteen chapters are written from the standpoint of the centrality of the resurrection of the dead in Jesus Christ in I Cor., ch. 15. The resurrection of Jesus Christ is the foundation of the church (ch. 15:1–11) and it is that without which all preaching and all faith are vain (ch. 15:12–34). It is the *sine qua non* of all gatherings of Christians together and of all that they do in their meetings, including their eating and drinking together. The risen, present Lord is the presupposition, not the effect or result of their eating and drinking. Moreover, what is done in Christian assemblies, including eating and drinking, must be done in a way that corresponds to and reflects the tremendous central event of all history, namely, the raising of the crucified Christ from the dead. In view of the resurrection it is unthinkable that Paul would advance a doctrine of the Lord's Supper in which Jesus would be made present or re-presented. Of course, "if Christ has not been raised," it would be necessary to invent sacraments that would recall a dead Savior and would communicate the benefits of his body and blood. But as "the breaking of bread" in Acts 2:42–47 presupposed the resurrection of Jesus Christ and the outpouring of the Holy Spirit, so the Lord's Supper in I Cor., ch. 11, presupposed the resurrection in ch. 15 and the gift of the Spirit in ch. 12.

Therefore, when Paul reminded the Corinthians that "the Lord Jesus on the night when he was betrayed took bread . . . and said, 'This is my body which is for you [or, broken for you],'" the meaning cannot be that in, with, and under the bread Christ's body is either realistically or spiritually eaten. When he took the cup and said, "This cup is the new covenant in my blood," the meaning cannot be that in, with, and under wine, Christ's blood is either realistically or spiritually drunk. Paul himself gives the correct interpretation when he explains that it is an action that is in remembrance of Jesus and is a proclamation of his death.

In order to determine *what* was eaten at the Last Supper as recorded in Matt. 26:26–29, Mark 14:22–25, and Luke 22:15–20, 27–30, we should perhaps decide whether the Last Supper was a Passover or the Lord's Supper or both. If it were the Lord's Supper as observed in The Acts of the Apostles and in I Corinthians, it would have been an ordinary meal consisting of all kinds of food and drink, including bread and wine. If, however, it was a Passover meal, it consisted of *hors d'oeuvres* of green herbs, bitter herbs, and fruit sauce (*haroseth*), a mixture of dried fruits, spices, and vinegar, then unleavened bread and wine, and the main dish of roast lamb.[58] Although E. Schweizer believes that "the arguments against a Passover Meal seem more persuasive" and that theologically the question appears to be unimportant,[59] and although R. Fuller[60] and D. M. MacKinnon[61] conclude that a final decision is impossible, J. Jeremias, M. Barth and A. J. B. Higgins provide conclusive evidence, we believe, that the Last Supper was a Passover meal. We do not propose to review all the evidence here.

Exegetically of greatest importance are the instructions Jesus gave for the preparation for the Passover meal (Matt. 26:17–19; Mark 14:12–16; Luke 22:7–13), especially the words of Peter and John to the householder: "The Teacher says to you, Where is the guest room, where I am to eat the passover with my disciples?" (Luke 22:11) and Jesus' words: "I have earnestly desired to eat this passover with you before I suffer" (Luke 22:15). Theologically important is the fact that Jesus was "born under the law, to redeem those who were under the law" (Gal. 4:4–5) and had come not to abolish the law but to fulfill it (Matt. 5:17–19). Accordingly, we find it strange that Jeremias should argue that Jesus' first vow of abstinence "can only have come before the beginning of the meal, and the second immediately following, at the passing of the first cup. At the Last Supper, therefore, Jesus neither ate of the passover Lamb nor drank of the wine; probably he fasted completely." [62] On the contrary, the simple meaning seems to be that Jesus declared that after this Passover Meal he would not eat it again "until it is fulfilled in the kingdom of God" (Luke 22:16), "until the kingdom of God comes" (Luke 22:18). If Jesus had had no intention of eating the Passover, why had he said that he would "eat the passover with my disciples"? The fact is that Jesus fulfilled the law of Moses to the last iota, and then in his death did away with the Passover "by abolishing in his flesh the law of commandments and ordinances" (Eph. 2:15).

If the Last Supper was a Passover meal—the last Passover meal —and if Jesus ate it, then what he ate and drank was the food and drink described above. When, therefore, he "took bread" and "took a cup" and said: "This is my body" and "This is my blood," the meaning cannot be that he ate and drank himself. His eating and drinking the Passover can only be a figurative and anticipatory eating and drinking of *the* Passover Lamb, not in the Lord's Supper but in the crucifixion of Jesus Christ by men. Jesus Christ himself is the Passover Lamb (I Cor. 5:7; John 1:29, 36; I Peter 1:19; Rev. 13:8; 5:6 ff.; 7:9 f., 14; 12:11; 14:4). Even if we assume that Jesus abstained from eating and drinking, it cannot be maintained that the disciples ate and drank Christ's body and blood in and with bread, wine, and roast lamb *before* his death, *before* the lamb of God had been sacrificed. Moreover, after he had been sacrificed once and for all, the Lord's Supper could not be a repetition or extension of his sacrifice, of eating and drinking his flesh and blood. Concerning the meaning of Jesus' words, "This is my body" and "This is my blood," surely A. J. B. Higgins gives a correct interpretation when he writes:

The disciples at the Last Supper are not to be regarded as eating (symbolically) the flesh of Christ in partaking of the bread and as drinking his blood in taking the wine, but as remembering his sacrificial act. The real significance of the Passover lambs was that they *represented* the efficacious death of the lambs in Egypt—whether they were regarded as having effected atonement or solely deliverance of the Israelite households from the destroyer—but they possessed no efficacy themselves. In the same way the bread and the wine of the Eucharist *represent* the atoning sacrifice of Christ as the true paschal lamb without themselves possessing any inherent efficacy. . . . Both at the Passover and at the Eucharist the sacrificial death is presupposed and is no part of the actual meal. The Eucharist is therefore a proclamation and a remembrance of what has taken place—or rather of what God has done—just like the Passover. What is to be emphasized is not the eucharistic elements themselves, but the sacrificial act they call to mind.[63]

Although at the Last Supper the body and blood of Jesus were not eaten and drunk, it was a proleptic eating and drinking in remembrance of Jesus *as if* the Lamb of God had already been sacrificed. This is the probable explanation of Paul's addition of the words: "Do this in remembrance of me" and "As often as you eat this bread and drink the cup, you proclaim the Lord's death until he comes," and of the long text of Luke, in which are found the words: "Do this in remembrance of me" and "This cup which is poured out for you is the new covenant in my blood." [64]

It may be recalled that Cullmann has argued that the joyous "breaking of bread" by the first Christians in Acts is to be traced back to the resurrection meals with Jesus, whereas the Pauline doctrine of eating and drinking Jesus is to be traced back to the Last Supper and to the sad and mournful thoughts associated with his death. But this line of argumentation falls to the ground once it is recognized that the Last Supper, as a Passover meal, was itself a joyful meal. It celebrated the salvation of the firstborn from the avenging angel through the blood of the lamb sprinkled on the doorposts and the deliverance out of Egypt. The Passover meal was a joyous occasion because it was a thanksgiving meal. It celebrated not only something that had happened in the past but was a present reality. "One did not think of the lamb and its death but of the saving event for which the lamb, the bitter herbs and the unleavened bread were signs" (M. Barth). The Passover meal was not a dramatic presentation of the way in which the lamb had been slaughtered; it was an acknowledgment of God's gracious act of redemption. The fact that the disciples sang a hymn at the conclusion of the meal (Mark 14:26; Matt. 26:30) and that wine was used—"wine to gladden the heart of man" (Ps. 104:15)—are proofs that it was a festive occasion. True, the occasion was marred by the intimation of Judas' betrayal, by the agonizing question, "Is it I?" and by Jesus' announcement of his impending death. But the very fact that these things occurred in the context of the death of *the* Passover Lamb by which their sin and death would be overcome, is proof that the dominant note was one of joy. The death of Jesus was a triumphant death—the death of death! Actually the Passover was a pre-Easter Easter meal. It prefigured Christ's victorious death. We conclude, therefore, that there are not "two types of Eucharist" in the New Testament, but one joyous feast of thanksgiving, love, and hope in a remembrance and proclamation of Jesus.

Nevertheless, there is one single passage in the New Testament in which it is explicitly stated that the flesh and blood of Jesus must be eaten and drunk if men are to have life: John 6:51–58. The crucial question is whether this passage refers to a sacramental eating and drinking of the flesh and blood of Jesus, as most commentators (but not all!) contend. Because of its cruciality, the passage deserves careful reconsideration.[65]

The theme of the entire sixth chapter of John's Gospel is the bread of life. An analysis of the structure of the chapter reveals the following: (1) Verses 1–14 give the account of the feeding of the five thousand, in which Jesus, who is himself the true Bread, is manifested as the Giver of earthly food. (2) Verses 15–32 deal with the misunderstanding of the sign and of Jesus as the bread of life. (3) Verses 33–47 treat of the descent of the bread of life from heaven and of faith in him. This section is unquestionably the unifying center of the whole chapter. It is expanded in vs. 48–60 to show that (4) the bread of life is the flesh of the Son of God delivered up to death at the hands of men for the life of the world and to record the consequent unbelief of the Jews and the disciples. (5) Verses 61–62 speak of the ascension of the bread of life and the possibility of offense. Finally, (6), vs. 63–71 deal with the Spirit and the words of eternal life concerning the bread of life and with the ensuing offense and faith. Taken together, the six sections are concerned with a twofold movement: the descent of the Father's Son in the form of man into the depths of death, and the ascent of the Son of man to heaven, whence he had come. In this twofold movement and in the unity of the Son of God and Son of man, Jesus Christ is the *one* bread of life for the world in which men are called to believe. The one coherent and unified theme of John, ch. 6, is the pre-existent, incarnate, crucified, and ascended Jesus who is at once the Giver of earthly bread and the bread of life itself. With the possible exception of vs. 63–71 concerning the Spirit and the words of life, the chapter is exclusively Christological.

In his commentary *The Gospel According to John*, Raymond E. Brown enumerates the following theories that have been propounded concerning the structure of John 6:35–58:

(a) The whole discourse (vs. 35–58) refers to the revelation by and in Jesus or his teaching. This "sapiential" interpretation of 35–58 is championed by Godet, B. Weiss, Bornhäuser, Odeberg, Schlatter, Strathmann. (b) Only the first part of the discourse (35–50 or 35–51) has this theme, but in 51–58 the bread refers to the eucharistic flesh of Jesus. This half-and-half view has attracted Lagrange, E. Schweizer, Ménoud, Mollat, Mussner, Bultmann (the views of Dodd and Barrett also seem to imply two successive themes in the discourse). Many of these would regard 51–59 as a later addition. (c) The whole discourse (35–58) refers to eucharistic bread. Different shades of this view are supported by Loisy, Tobac, Buzy, Cullmann, Van den Busche. (d) The bread refers to *both* revelation and the eucharistic flesh of Jesus. Leon-Dufour sees these themes running through the discourse (35–58). Our view . . . sees the two themes in the first part of the discourse (35–50) which refers primarily to revelation but secondarily to the Eucharist, the second part (51–58) refers only to the Eucharist.

The chief objection to all these theories is the failure to recognize that Jesus Christ himself—in his unique person and work—is the *one* bread of life and that this *one* bread of life is the theme of the whole discourse of John 6:35–58. It is true that there are two sections in this discourse: (*a*) vs. 35–50 and (*b*) vs. 51–58. But it is overlooked that the passage about eating and drinking the flesh and blood is bracketed by the claim in v. 48 that "I am the bread of life" and by the assertion in v. 58 that "this is the bread which came down from heaven." The second of these sections explains *how* Jesus Christ is the bread of life of the world: he is the bread of life because he gives the flesh he has assumed as a sacrifice on the cross for the life of the world. The above theories suggest that the only flesh Jesus has is eucharistic flesh,

flesh given and received in the Eucharist. This would mean that when the Word became flesh (John 1:14), it became eucharistic flesh.

Brown argues for the "sapiential theme" in John 6:35–50 on the ground that the "bread of life" in this part of the discourse refers primarily to revelation in and by Jesus. It is true that the section deals with faith in Jesus Christ (vs. 35, 36, 40, 47) or of coming to him, which is a synonym for faith (vs. 35, 37, 44, 45). But bread is not a symbol for revelation and revelation is not the theme of the whole discourse. The symbol for revelation in John's Gospel is "light." To be sure, "the life was the light of men" (John 1:4). Jesus Christ is at once the work of salvation and the word of revelation. He reveals what he does and does what he reveals. But in John, ch. 6, the main emphasis is upon faith in the saving, life-giving *work* of Jesus. Brown also believes that "there is respectable evidence for holding that there is a secondary, eucharistic reference in 35–50, and this reference will become primary in 51–58." [66]

Let us note what Brown and others have done here. The correlate of revelation is said to be the Eucharist. Jesus is said to be the revelation as the bread of life. He is the life and the bread of life, not in himself, but only as his flesh and blood are eaten and drunk in the Eucharist. But revelation-Eucharist is an impossible correlation. It confuses Christology and ecclesiology. The correct correlation is revelation-salvation, light-life, word-work—both in Jesus Christ himself and in him alone—in *his* death and resurrection. Jesus is at once the light and the life of the world, quite apart from any preaching of the gospel through Word and sign, quite apart from the gift of food and drink, and quite apart from any eating and drinking. Whatever may be the form and content of the Lord's Supper, it is by no means on the same level as God's once-and-for-all word and work, revelation and salvation in the death and resurrection of Jesus Christ.

"I am the bread of life." (John 6:35,48,51.) But what is the bread which, according to John, Jesus claims to be? It is obviously not created, earthly bread, bread from below, which is the fruit of the earth and for which men labor (v. 27). It is not food such as Jesus distributed to the multitude from the five loaves and two fishes (vs. 9–11). Nor is it created heavenly bread such as the manna which the fathers ate in the wilderness—for they still died (vs. 31, 49). Finally, the bread of life is not some supposedly sacramental bread which Jesus is said to be in, with, and under. The bread of life is *Jesus Christ himself!* Nowhere is it suggested that in, with, and under the manna, or in, with, and under the loaves and the fish, Jesus gave himself to be eaten. And in the critical passage of vs. 51–58 there is no mention of elements in, with and under which Jesus' flesh and blood are eaten and drunk. If, then, Jesus is not earthly, heavenly, or sacramental bread, how are we to understand the "bread of life"? The bread of life is "the bread of God . . . which comes down from heaven, and gives life to the world" (v. 33). Jesus did not will to have or to be life only in and for himself. He wanted to share with the creature the life he already shared with the Father and the Spirit. He wanted to become the bread of life for the world (vs. 33, 51). Therefore, he is the bread of God which "comes down from heaven and gives life to the world" (vs. 33, 41, 42, 50, 51, 58). The bread became man in the person of "Jesus, the son of Joseph, whose father and mother we know" (v. 42). Jesus is the bread of life in that he assumed sinful, human flesh. More than that: he became and is the bread of life because he gives the flesh he has assumed as a sacrifice on the cross. The world has life only because Jesus has taken upon himself the flesh of men that is judged, sentenced, and condemned to die. In him the sentence of death upon all men is executed for all men. He gives his flesh to be lifted up on the cross as Moses lifted up the serpent in the wilderness that "whoever believes in him may have eternal life" (John 3:15; cf. chs. 8:28; 12:34). He gives up his flesh for the life of the world once and for all, wholly and completely. No other sacrifice is necessary to complete his self-offering. It can have no repetitions, no reenactments as in the Mystery religions.

We come now to John 6:51–58. It will be our contention that a sacrament or mystery has been imported into the exegesis of these verses, not only to bolster a sacramental view of the church and its ministry, but also to explain, and explain away, "the hard saying" about which "the Jews then disputed among themselves, saying, 'How can this man give us his flesh to eat?'" (v. 52) and

at which the disciples murmured and took offense (v. 61). Bultmann believes that the passage is a later redaction by an editor,
possibly under the influence of the Mystery religions.[67] If that
were the case, we might dismiss the passage as contrary to the
witness of the rest of the New Testament. Then we would be
rid of the problem. That won't do; we take it as an authentic
testimony of John to a truth enunciated by Jesus. (We do not
insist that they are the *ipsissima verba* of Jesus.) We begin with
several general observations.

1. In the passage there is no mention of bread and wine as
visible signs of the body and blood. True, bread is mentioned;
but it is "the bread which came down from heaven."

2. There are no words of institution, breaking of bread, giving
thanks, and distribution of bread as means by which the body and
blood are said to be re-presented and conveyed.

3. There is no technical or liturgical explanation of *how* men
eat and drink Christ's body and blood, no pat sacramental answer
to the question: "How can this man give us his flesh to eat?"

4. The parallelism between ch. 4 concerning the water of life
and ch. 6 concerning the bread of life has been noted by many
commentators. But why was not a sacrament brought in to explain
how one "drinks" the water of life? If a sacrament is not necessary
to explain how one drinks the water of eternal life which Jesus
gives, why is it necessary to explain how one "eats" the bread of
life?

5. Even if we grant for a moment that a sacramental eating
and drinking of Jesus is described in John 6:51–58, we dare not
think that the sacrament is absolutely necessary in order to appropriate the bread of life or even that there is a twofold appropria-
tion by the sacrament *and* by faith. It is explicitly and repeatedly
stated that faith is the one work by which we obtain "the food
that endures to eternal life." According to John, the *one* human
response to both the objective and subjective work of reconciliation and salvation in Jesus Christ and the Holy Spirit is faith (John
3:36; 4:39, 41; 5:24; 6:29, 35, 36, 40, 47, 64, 69). Most significant is the fact that the necessity for faith in the words is stressed
again *after* the discourse about eating and drinking the flesh and
blood of the Son of man (John 6:64 f.). The whole passage of

John 6:48–58 is bracketed by the statement: "He who believes has eternal life." If faith is the one work required of men, then a sacramental eating and drinking is superfluous.

6. It is not said that the eating and drinking of the flesh and blood is a sacrament for the elect or for believing Christians or for those who partake of the Lord's Supper. It is the event of Jesus' giving his flesh *for the world.*

7. Those who oppose a sacramental interpretation of John 6:51–58 usually interpret the eating and drinking of the flesh and blood as equivalent to a spiritual eating and drinking by faith. We wish to suggest, however, that the passage may be interpreted as being descriptive of an *objective* eating and drinking of the flesh and blood that is not a sacramental action.

"The Jews then disputed [argued] among themselves, saying, 'How can this man give us his flesh to eat?' " (John 6:52.) It is important to see clearly that the question about which the Jews debated was related strictly to Jesus' statement: "The bread which I shall give for the life of the world is my flesh." It is related to the question *how* Jesus will give his flesh as a sacrifice. In what manner will his sacrificial death be accomplished? Will he commit suicide like Samson? Will he deliver his body to be burned? (I Cor. 13:3.) Will he cast himself down from the pinnacle of the Temple? (Matt. 4:5 f.) Will he die by leading a revolt against the Romans? (Mark 15:7.) It is equally important to see that Jesus' answer is related strictly to his own statement about giving his flesh for the life of the world. Jesus does not answer a question about which Christians quarreled years later, namely, how the body and blood of Jesus are eaten and drunk in the Eucharist after Jesus had died and risen again. Such a question could never have entered their minds *before* his death and resurrection, and the Jews could never have understood Jesus' answer if it had been a reference to a future institution of a sacramental Eucharist. For a sacramental eating and drinking of flesh and blood is foreign to the Old Testament. The question of the Jews and Jesus' answer have to do with the way in which Jesus will offer up his flesh for the life of the world.

The answer Jesus gives is that he will offer up his flesh by the Jews eating his flesh and blood. Jesus will give himself up to death—it will be a voluntary sacrifice on his part—but he will do so at the hands of men.[68] They will become guilty of murdering him. (Cf. Acts 2:23, 36; 3:15; 4:10; 5:30; 7:52; 10:39; 13:28.) The Jews will live only by putting Jesus to death.

Is eating flesh and drinking blood an appropriate way to describe the way in which Jesus will die? It is an apt description, not only of the violent, hostile way in which men put Jesus to death, but also of the effect of his death upon his enemies. In the Bible "to eat someone's flesh" is a metaphor for a hostile action. "When the wicked, even mine enemies and my foes, came upon me to eat up my flesh, they stumbled and fell." (Ps. 27:2, KJV.) The psalmist complains that evildoers "eat up my people as they eat bread" (Ps. 14:4; cf. Ps. 53:4). The cry of dereliction, "My God, my God, why hast thou forsaken me?" is quoted by Jesus from Ps. 22, evidently because "strong bulls . . . open wide their mouths at me, like a ravening and roaring lion" (Ps. 22:12 f. cf. Ps. 22:16; 57:4). So the psalmist prays: "Deliver my soul from the sword, my life from the power of the dog! Save me from the mouth of the lion" (Ps. 22:20 f.). And in Ps. 35:25: "Let them not say, 'We have swallowed him up' " and in Ps. 59:2: "Save me from bloodthirsty men" (cf. vs. 14 f.).

In his commentary *The Gospel According to John*, Raymond E. Brown refers to the passages we have quoted from the Old Testament as indicative of a "violent, hostile action." He adds that in Jer. 46:10 the symbolical meaning of drinking blood was that of brutal slaughter, and that in Ezekiel's vision of apocalyptic carnage (Ezek. 39:17) the scavenger birds are invited to come to the feast: "You shall eat flesh and drink blood." Brown concludes: "Thus if Jesus' words in [John] 6:53 are to have a favorable meaning, they must refer to the Eucharist." He further suggests that the use of *trōgein*, which originally refers to eating by animals and which may be rendered "gnaw" or "munch" is "part of John's attempt to emphasize the realism of the eucharistic flesh and blood." It is strange, indeed, that he has seen the fulfillment of these Old Testament passages in a sacramental Eucharist and not in the manner of Christ's crucifixion.

What is portrayed in these Old Testament passages, and also in John 6:53–58, is an eating of "flesh with its life, that is, its blood" (Gen. 9:3 f.) which, as we have already noted, was strictly forbidden in the law. The life of Jesus is his blood, and it becomes our life only as it is shed by men. That is the *effect* of the shedding of his blood. That is the objective eating and drinking of his flesh and blood, and faith is the subjective acknowledgment and confession that we are guilty of having murdered the Righteous One (cf. Acts 2:23; 7:52). No wonder many of Jesus' disciples exclaimed: "This is a hard saying; who can listen to it?" The translation of the New English Bible, while certainly not literal, captures the revulsion: "This is more than we can stomach! Why listen to such words?" No wonder the disciples "murmured" and were scandalized (John 6:61)! The offense here is not merely an offense to reason at the alleged mystery of the communication of Christ's body and blood in bread and wine; it is the scandal of the cross. "We preach Christ crucified, a stumbling block to Jews and folly to Gentiles." (I Cor. 1:23.)

John 6:56 is frequently taken to mean that the abiding of men in Jesus and of him in them is a result or effect of their eating and drinking his flesh and blood in the Eucharist. Actually what Jesus is saying is that in spite of men crucifying and consuming his flesh, they nevertheless remain in him and he in them. Men may think that they have finally gotten rid of Jesus by putting him to death (cf. Matt. 21:38 f. and par.). But their union with him established in the incarnation cannot be broken by his death! Why? Because the flesh which Jesus delivered up into the hands of wicked men was *our flesh* which he had assumed. Secondly, as the following verse explains, their union with him cannot be broken because Jesus lives because of the Father. Therefore: "He who eats me will live because of me" (John 6:57). "Because I live you will live also . . . [because] I am in my Father, and you in me, and I in you" (John 14:19 f.).[69]

John 6:62–71 speaks about the ascension of the Son of man, about the life-giving Spirit, and about the unbelief of the disciples. When Jesus had previously said, "Unless you eat the flesh of the Son of man and drink his blood, you have no life in you," he did not mean that a life-giving power is immanent in the flesh as such. Not the incarnate flesh of Jesus, and certainly not a supposedly eucharistic flesh, is life-giving. "The flesh is of no avail" (v. 63).

It can do nothing of itself. Only as the Son of man is raised from death by the Spirit is it life-giving. "It is the Spirit that gives life" (v. 63; cf. Rom. 1:4; 8:11; II Cor. 3:6). Because the Spirit gives life to the mortal flesh of the Son of man, the words he has spoken are "spirit and life."

"But there are some of you that do not believe. . . . After this many of his disciples drew back and no longer went about with him" (John 6:64, 66). At the beginning of this chapter in John's Gospel there were five thousand who were ready to take Jesus and make him their king. At the end there were twelve, and one of them was a traitor. To these twelve Jesus said: "Will you also go away?" Simon Peter, the very disciple who rebuked Jesus for deciding to go up to Jerusalem to suffer many things and to be killed, the same Peter who was to deny him thrice—this disciple, speaking for the others who were offended in him and who in the end forsook him and fled, said: "Lord, to whom shall we go? You have the words [not now the bread, or the flesh and blood, but words *about them*] of eternal life; and we have believed and have come to know that you are the Holy One of God" (v. 68 f.). Herein is the miracle of the church which, founded upon these twelve, believes and confesses that Jesus is Israel's Messiah and the Bread of life for the world.

John, ch. 6, in agreement with Paul and the Synoptists, describes a once-and-for-all descent of the Son of man from the Father and from heaven (v. 33), a once-and-for-all assumption of the flesh in the birth of Jesus of Joseph and Mary (v. 42), a once-and-for-all giving of his flesh for the life of the world (v. 51), a once-and-for-all eating of the bread of life which is his flesh and blood (vs. 51 ff.), and a once-and-for-all ascension where he was before (v. 62). It is the ascension that definitely rules out a repetition of the incarnation, passion, and death of Jesus, and a repetition of eating and drinking his flesh and blood unto eternal life. To be sure, Jesus comes again in the Spirit, but not to suffer and die again, not to have his enemies come upon him to eat up his flesh. Now in the unity of his divine and human, humiliated and exalted person, he is present with his church in the Spirit. Hence, as often as we eat and drink *with* him who is the Bread of life, we do it in *remembrance* of what he has already done for us, in *remembrance* of the shed blood of the covenant, and we *proclaim* his death until he comes. Once again we conclude that there is no justification for the view that two types of the Eucharist are to be found in the New Testament. There is one joyous meal of faith, love, and hope—a meal eaten and drunk in fellowship with the risen, present Lord.

The answer to the question to which this appendix has been addressed, namely, whether Jesus is eaten in the Lord's Supper, has been given. There is no evidence whatever in the New Testament of a sacramental eating of Jesus. It is a view that arose in the first centuries of the church under the influence of the Greek Mystery religions. It is a relic of pagan animism, magic, and superstition which has no place in the New Testament and should be given no place in the church. But that is not the main reason it should be banished. The main reason is that it derogates from Jesus Christ as the *one* Mediator, the *one* means of grace and faith.

Appendix II.

THE CASE OF
"THE UGLY, BROAD DITCH" AND
THE LEUENBERG AGREEMENT OF 1973

Sacramentalism is basically the view that the church's ministry is the means by which Christ is made cognitively and savingly present and available to men. Although the church has always affirmed the omnipresence and contemporaneity of Jesus Christ, the view has prevailed that God's saving work in Jesus Christ has been imprisoned by the limitations of space and time, so that he cannot really be with men here and now and they cannot be with him, unless his presence is somehow made real, realized, re-presented, repeated, fulfilled or extended by the church's own ministry. The church was faced—or thought it was faced—with the problem of making Christ and his benefits or merits contemporaneous. He had ascended into heaven and in his supposed absence the church imagined that it had to be the means or channel of making him savingly present through its own ministry of Word and sacraments, and therefore that it had to be the "mediatrix of salvation." The church virtually ceased to believe in Christ's presence and imminent return except through its own activity. Because of his supposed absence and delay of the parousia, preaching and the sacraments came to be regarded as "the means of grace" by which the "real presence" of Christ and his benefits were achieved.

Actually the church thought it was faced with the problem that troubled the philosopher Gotthold Ephraim Lessing (1729–1781). While accepting the prevailing view that there is what he called "the ugly, broad ditch" between Christ's resurrection and us, he was not satisfied that the church had bridged the gap and had made Christ present after eighteen hundred years. Lessing spoke of "the ugly, broad ditch which I cannot get across, however often and however earnestly I have tried to make the leap. If anyone can help me over it, let him do it, I beg him, I adjure him. He will have a divine reward from me." [1] Lessing's question, as rephrased by Barth, was, how can we be reached and affected by what happened back then. "How can that which happened once even if it did happen for us, be recognized today as having happened for us, seeing it does not happen today? . . . How can that which happened once have happened for us when we who live today were not there and could not experience it ourselves." Lessing could not make the leap because of his belief that "accidental truths of history can never become the proof of necessary truths of reason." [3] The resurrection of Christ as a past event cannot prove the truth (of reason) that he is the Son of God. Lessing had to have firsthand, personal experience of miracles, and not just historical reports of them, if a proof of Jesus Christ is to be afforded.

Assuming that there is an "ugly, broad ditch" between the time of Jesus Christ and our time, theologians have availed themselves of a number of ways of bridging it and making Christ contemporaneous. The first is that of idealism, namely, that the historical facts of religion do not matter; what is important are the timeless ideas of truth, beauty, and goodness which the facts illustrate. Obviously this solution robbed Christianity of its historical roots and reduced it to a myth. Søren Kierkegaard devoted two chapters of Book Two of *Concluding Unscientific Postscript* to Lessing. [4] He argued that the historical is the *occasion* and God himself is the *condition* whereby "the leap of faith" makes one a genuine contemporary of Jesus—a thought he had explored in *Philosophical Fragments*. In a sense Karl Barth's early doctrine of the unity of the threefold form of God's Word as revealed, written, and preached was another attempt to bridge the "ugly, broad ditch." The revealed Word, which is Jesus Christ incarnate, is present in the preached Word. In his book *Wort und Glaube* (1960; E.T. *Word and Faith*, 1963), Gerhard Ebeling contends that hermeneutics is the question how the unique historical revelation becomes a present actuality. In the essay entitled "The Significance of the Critical Historical Method for Church and Theology in Protestantism," he offers a solution in line with a Lutheran-Kierkegaardian concept of faith, whereas in a later essay on "Word of God and Hermeneutics," stress is laid upon "word-event" (Wort- and Sprach-Ereignis) as the means of bridging the gap. In the former essay Ebeling rejects various Roman Catholic and Protestant solutions of actualizing revelation, such as the identi-fication of revelation with Holy Scripture, and imitative histori-cizing by means of drama, ordering of the church year, and the use of relics and pilgrimages.

One of the most important sections in the whole of Karl Barth's *Church Dogmatics* is the section in the doctrine of recon-ciliation entitled "The Verdict of the Father." [5] There Barth car-ries on a quiet debate not only with Lessing and with the theology of G. Thomasius[6] and R. Bultmann, but with the traditional un-derstanding of Christology in Roman Catholicism and Protes-tantism. It affords the deepest reason for his rejection of sacra-mentalism. Barth came to see that the New Testament speaks of the life, death, and resurrection of Jesus not as an ideal, principle, or potentiality that has to be subsequently realized and actualized but as a concrete deed of God in time that has radically altered the situation of all men in all times and places. For that reason Lessing's assumption of an "ugly, broad ditch" of eighteen hun-dred years was a *false* assumption and the question of leaping over it was a spurious question. There was no ditch that had to be bridged for the simple reason that no ditch existed. The event of the incarnation (which embraces Christ's death and resurrection!) is the event in which God's space and time assumed creaturely space and time into unity with itself, so that there is no time and place where God in Christ is not contemporaneous with man. "For 'in him we live and move and have our being.'" (Acts 17:28.)

The resurrection of Jesus Christ is God's declaration and desig-nation, God's proof, that he who came from the seed of David has been designated or declared to be the Son of God, and there-fore, the one who is not a prisoner of a dead past or of a past death, but who is alive and present forever more. The fact that

Jesus Christ is present as the creative and reconciling word and work of God once and for all times, whether men know it or not, does not preclude, however, his special presence by the Holy Spirit so that men may believe and confess his preserving and reconciling presence. But the faith of the church, its preaching and sacraments, cannot and need not realize Christ's presence. "The confession of Christians, their suffering, their repentance, their prayer, their humility, their works, baptism too, and the Lord's Supper can and should attest this event but only attest it. The event itself, the event of the death of man, is that of the death of Jesus Christ on Golgotha: no other event, no earlier and no later, no event which simply prepares the way for it, no effect which has to give to it the character of an actual event. This is the one *mysterium*, the one sacrament, and the one existential fact before and after which there is no room for any other of the same rank." [7] "The event of the incarnation . . . is the great Christian mystery and sacrament beside which there is, in the strict and proper sense, no other." [8]

Because there is no "ugly, broad ditch," because Jesus Christ is present as God's justification of sinful men, because that justification is valid for men here and now, and because Jesus is specially present in the power of the Holy Spirit so that men may be subjectively "justified by faith alone," it is evident that we can no longer concur in the sacramentalism of the Lutheran and Reformed confessions of the sixteenth century. Nor can we concur in the concessions which the Leuenberg Agreement of 1973 has made to sacramentalism.

A preliminary draft of the Leuenberg Agreement was drawn up by representatives of Lutheran, Reformed, and United Churches in Europe, and was submitted to the respective churches for their criticisms and reactions. Reactions to the first drafts were said to have been "generally favorable." The final draft was prepared in March, 1973, at a meeting which was attended by fifty-one representatives from churches in sixteen countries. The work has been under the joint auspices of the Faith and Order Secretariat of the World Council of Churches, the Lutheran World Federation, and the World Alliance of Reformed Churches. The ongoing theological conversations recommended by the Leuenberg Agreement will be sponsored by the LWF and the WARC. The earlier draft was also studied in the second round of the Lutheran-Reformed conversations in the United States. (At the conclusion of the first round in February, 1966, the Report to the Sponsoring Confessional Organizations stated: "As a result of our studies and discussions we see no insuperable obstacles to pulpit and altar fellowship and, therefore, we recommend to our parent bodies that they encourage their constituent churches to enter into discussions looking forward to intercommunion and the fuller recognition of one another's ministries" [*Marburg Revisited*; Augsburg Publishing House, 1966, p. 191].) The text of the Leuenberg Agreement has been sent to ninety Lutheran, Reformed, and United Churches in Europe for adoption.

The purpose of the Leuenberg Agreement is to achieve a church fellowship by means of a pulpit and table fellowship which includes a mutual recognition of ordination and intercommunion. The Agreement does not confess any errors that may have been committed by the Lutheran and Reformed churches. On the contrary, "the Agreement leaves intact the binding force of the confessions within the participating churches. It is not to be regarded as a new confession of faith. It sets forth a consensus reached about central matters, one which makes church fellowship possible between churches of different confessional positions" (35b). According to the Agreement, "the differences which from the time of the Reformation onwards have made church fellowship between the Lutheran and Reformed Churches impossible and have led them to pronounce mutual condemnations are related to the doctrine of the Lord's Supper, Christology, and the doctrine of predestination" (17). On the basis of its statements about these doctrines, the Agreement holds that "the condemnations of the Reformation Confessions . . . are inapplicable to the doctrinal position. This does not mean that the condemnations pronounced by the Reformation fathers are irrelevant; but they are no longer an obstacle to Church fellowship" (26).

Now one can concur with the Leuenberg Agreement when it declares: "The fundamental witness to the Gospel is the testimony of the apostles and prophets in the Holy Scriptures of the Old and New Testaments. It is the task of the Church to spread this

Gospel by the spoken word in preaching, by individual counseling, and by Baptism and the Lord's Supper" (13). We can also agree that "when we celebrate the Lord's Supper we proclaim the death of Christ through which God has reconciled the world with himself. We proclaim the presence of the risen Lord in our midst. Rejoicing that the Lord has come to us we await his future coming in glory" (16). But we cannot agree that "*in* preaching, Baptism and the Lord's Supper, Jesus Christ is present through the Holy Spirit" (13). (The preliminary draft read: "*Through* preaching, Baptism and the Lord's Supper Jesus Christ is present in the Holy Spirit.") We cannot agree that "*in* baptism Jesus Christ irrevocably receives man, fallen prey to sin and death, into his fellowship of salvation so that he may become a new creature" (14a), nor that "*in* the Lord's Supper Jesus Christ imparts himself in his body and blood, given up for all, through his word of promise with bread and wine" (14b; cf. 18). We cannot agree that "we cannot separate communion with Jesus Christ in his body and blood from the act of eating and drinking" (19), and that "in the sacraments, the Holy Spirit, and so God himself, makes the crucified and risen Jesus present to us" (21). Still less can we agree that "justification in Christ is *thus* imparted to men and *in this way* the Lord gathers his people" (13) and "he *thereby* grants us forgiveness of sins and sets us free for a new life of faith" (14b).

We cannot accept these statements because they contradict what the Leuenberg Agreement itself had previously declared, namely, that "through *his* Word, God by his Holy Spirit calls all men to repent and *believe*, and assures the *believing* sinner of his righteousness in Jesus Christ. Whoever puts his *trust* in the Gospel is justified in God's sight for the sake of Jesus Christ and set free from the accusation of the law" (10c). (Italics have been added to the above quotations.) Here Leuenberg rightly affirms that we are justified by faith alone in Jesus Christ through the immediate work of the Holy Spirit. The wonderful virtues, powers, and effects, which the Leuenberg Agreement later ascribes to the sacraments, are also contradicted by its statement that "the unique mediation of Jesus Christ in salvation is the heart of the Scriptures" (12e). (The German text might also be translated:

"The exclusive saving mediatorship of Jesus Christ is the heart of Scripture.") But apparently for Leuenberg Jesus is not really the *one* Mediator of grace and faith: he himself has to be mediated by Baptism and the Lord's Supper. Thus in this view the church is the mediatrix of justification, of the forgiveness of sins, of freedom for a new life, and therefore of salvation. Not Jesus Christ and the Spirit, but the church and its ministry through the sacraments is the bridge over the supposed "ugly, broad ditch"!

Laudable as are all efforts to achieve union, or at least intercommunion among Christians, it is a pity that the framers of the Leuenberg Agreement sought agreement on the basis of a sacramentalism that was common to the Lutheran and Reformed traditions of the sixteenth century. It is unfortunate that they did not reexamine the whole question of sacraments, especially when sacraments are being called in question today by New Testament and systematic theologians.

Notes and References

Chapter 1. WHY MEN MAY EAT AND DRINK WITH JESUS

1. The commandment to eat and drink is not to be regarded as a timeless, universally valid principle. As the commandment to live is not unconditional, and since a man may be commanded to surrender his life, so a man may be commanded to fast, even unto death. One thinks immediately of Jesus' forty-day fast in the wilderness (Matt. 4:1 f.; Luke 4:1 f.) and his fast until death after he had eaten the Passover for the last time with his disciples (Luke 22:16, 18; cf. Matt. 26:29; Mark 14:25). One recalls the private fasts of Moses because of the sins of the Israelites (Deut. 9:9, 18), of Elijah (I Kings 19:8), of David (II Sam. 12:16–23) and of Esther (Esth. 4:15–17), and the public fasts proclaimed by Jehoiakim (Jer. 36:9 f.), by Ezra (Ezra 8:21 f.), and by Nehemiah (Neh. 9:1 ff.), and the fasts called for in the books of Jonah (ch. 3:5–9) and Joel (chs. 1:13 f.; 2:12). One recalls the fact that the disciples of John the Baptist and of the Pharisees fasted, whereas Jesus' disciples did not. Fasting is a sign of sin, sickness, and death, of godly sorrow, mourning, and repentance, a sign of God's judgment and wrath. Eating and drinking, on the other hand, are signs of justification and sanctification, of reconciliation and peace, of resurrection and life, of thanksgiving and joy. Although only one meal is said to have been a "breakfast," all eating and drinking by the risen Christ was a breaking of his fast unto death.

2. John tells us that it was on "the other side of the sea of Galilee which is the sea of Tiberias." Luke presents a problem when he states that Jesus and the disciples "withdrew apart to a city called Bethsaida." To confuse it more, Mark has the disciples crossing to Bethsaida after the miracle (Mark 6:45). Perhaps the difficulty may be resolved if we assume that the miracle occurred as they were on the way to Bethsaida.

3. Cf. B. A. Mastin, "Jesus Said Grace," *Scottish Journal of Theology*, Vol. 24, p. 451, and J. Jeremias, *The Eucharistic Words of Jesus*, p. 176.

4. H. L. Strack and P. Billerbeck, *Kommentar zum Neuen Testament aus Talmud und Midrasch* (Munich: C. H. Becksche Verlagsbuchhandlung, 1922–), Vol. II, pp. 246 f. It was a strict rule for a Jew that he should eat nothing before a blessing is pronounced. All benedictions begin with the words: "Blessed be thou, O Lord our God, King of the world." The blessing of a meal including wine would continue: "who hast caused bread to come forth out of the earth and who hast created the fruit of the vine." According to Hermann W. Beyer, "in common meals the main part is opened with a blessing usually pronounced by the head of the house with a piece of bread in his hand. The others confirm it with an Amen. After this the head of the house breaks the bread and distributes to those who sit at table with him." (Art. "εὐλογέω," etc., R. Kittel, ed., *Theological Dictionary of the New Testament* [Wm. B. Eerdmans Publishing Company, 1964–], Vol. II, p. 760; cf. Strack-Billerbeck, Vol. IV, pp. 616 ff.; G. Dalman, *Jesus-Jeschua* [1922], p. 123.)

5. Beyer states that "it is a Gk. misunderstanding of the Aram. original that many MSS add an acc. object (αὐτά or ταῦτα) at Mk. 8:7. If this suggests the idea that Jesus blessed the bread and thus made possible its miraculous increase, we have a relapse into a conception long since left behind in Israel." (*Ibid.*, p. 762.)

6. Johannes Behm, art. "κλάω," *Theological Dictionary of the New Testament*, Vol. III, pp. 728 f.

7. From Jesus' fivefold action not a few scholars have sought to derive the liturgy of the Lord's Supper (e.g., Gregory Dix, *The Shape of the Liturgy*, p. 48; G. D. Kilpatrick, *Remaking the Liturgy*, p. 34; and John A. T. Robinson, *Liturgy Coming to Life,*

The Westminster Press, 1965). It is claimed that Jesus' action in feeding the multitudes was "eucharistic." In his commentary on *The Gospel According to John* (The Anchor Bible, Vols. 29 [i–xii] and 29a [xiii–xxi]; Doubleday & Company, Inc., 1966, 1970; see Vol. 29, pp. 240–243), Raymond E. Brown has provided a chart showing the parallels between the Johannine and Synoptic accounts of the feedings and the Last Supper in the Synoptics. Now such parallels are not surprising, since these actions are necessarily performed at any Jewish or Christian meal. There is always a taking of food, giving thanks, dividing it, and giving it to those at table. Certainly the feedings of the multitudes were "eucharistic" in that they were meals at which and for which Jesus gave thanks. Unfortunately this is not what some scholars mean by "eucharistic." They mean a sacrament or cultic rite which becomes efficacious through the repetition of the fivefold words or acts of institution whereby Christ's body and blood are said to be present. It seems arbitrary to read this meaning of "eucharistic" back into the feedings of the multitudes or into the meal which Paul urged all on board to take during the storm at sea in Acts 27:33–38. Scholars have debated whether the passage in Acts refers to the Eucharist or (as some recent commentators have contended: F. F. Bruce, E. Haenchen, C. S. C. Williams) to Paul's observance of the Jewish custom of saying grace before meals. M. Wilcox has claimed that "although the original act recorded in Acts 27:35 may not have been eucharistic, yet the temptation to invest it with a certain eucharistic significance was not easy to resist" (*The Semitisms of Acts* [Oxford University Press, 1965], p. 82). To which B. A. Mastin (*loc. cit.*, p. 434) has replied: "At most, phraseology which Wilcox says is 'clearly reminiscent of the language of the Words of Institution of the Eucharist' may indicate that Jesus was thought to be present with his followers whenever bread was broken; certainly seen in context the verse can only mean that Paul persuades men who are near exhaustion to take some nourishment by himself eating bread." Bo Reicke has argued that Paul could have presided only at a "prefiguration" of the Eucharist ("Die Mahlzeit mit Paulus auf den Wellen des Mittelmeers," *Theologische Zeitschrift*, Vol. IV [1948], pp. 401–410), whereas G. Wainwright is convinced that it was a Eucharist (*Eucharist and Eschatology*, pp. 130 f.). The answer to the question depends upon what is meant by "Eucharist." A meal that is eaten as an act of thanksgiving, love, and hope, especially when it is accompanied by the preaching of the good news (Acts 27:22–24), is a Eucharist. Paul encouraged the others to eat, not only to sustain their bodies but to sustain themselves in the hope of a future salvation when not a hair of any would perish. The meal combined thanksgiving, the apostle's love and concern for all on board (many of whom were presumably heathen sailors and passengers), and hope for salvation when all hope had been abandoned (Acts 27:20b). It was an ordinary meal by which physical bodies were sustained, and at the same time it pointed to the grace of salvation from death and the powers of evil, symbolized by the angry sea.

8. Cf. Ex. 24:15; Deut. 31:16; Ps. 73:27; Isa. 54:5; Ezek., ch. 16; Hos. 2:19 ff.; II Cor. 11:2; Eph. 5:22; Rev. 19:7 ff.; 21:2, 9; 22:17; Rom. 11:17 ff.; Eph. 2:19.

9. For the exposition that follows, cf. a sermon by Karl Barth on Luke 5:1–11 in *Die grosse Barmherzigkeit. Predigten* von Karl Barth und Eduard Thurneysen (Munich: Chr. Kaiser Verlag, 1935).

10. Edwyn Hoskyns, *The Fourth Gospel*, ed. by Francis Noel Davey, rev. ed. (Faber & Faber, Ltd., 1947), p. 326.

11. Walter Lüthi, *St. John's Gospel: An Exposition*, tr. by Kurt Schoenenberger (London: Oliver & Boyd, Ltd., 1960), pp. 86 f.

12. " 'What must we do, to be doing the works of God?' Jesus answered them, 'This is the work of God, that you believe in him whom he has sent.' " (John 6:28 f.) This passage might be taken to mean that faith is a divine work. But this would contradict explicit statements that faith is a work that men may and must do. Nowhere in Scripture is it said that God believes or that the Holy Spirit believes. Accordingly we take the phrase, τοῦτό ἐστιν τὸ ἔργον τοῦ θεοῦ, to refer back to the work of God the Father setting his seal upon the Son of man (John 6:27).

13. A detailed discussion of *how* men eat the bread of life, and of *how* they eat and drink the flesh and blood of the Son of man, will be found in Appendix I of this book.

14. Jesus goes to the Father only by going to his death, and in his death he was glorified. It is the risen, ascended Lord who gives the Holy Spirit (John 7:39; 13:3; 14:12, 28; 16:7; 17:1, 4 f.; 20:19, 22; Acts 1:4; 2:1, 4, 13, 15–17). The fact that Pentecost chronologically succeeded the death, resurrection, and ascension of Jesus is a sign that the gift of the Spirit is theologically dependent upon his death. But it does not preclude outpourings of the Spirit historically prior to Christ's death. Nevertheless, the outpouring of the Spirit upon all flesh, that is, upon Gentiles as well as Jews, marked the birth of the church as the fruit of Christ's death and resurrection.

15. In Jeremiah, Isaiah, Ezekiel, and Habakkuk we read of a cup that God hands to the nations and even forces them to drink. It is the cup of the wine of his wrath, and the effect of it is to make the peoples stagger and reel like drunken men. It is what Isaiah calls "the bowl of staggering" (Isa. 51:17). According to Jeremiah, " 'Thus says the LORD of hosts, the God of Israel: Drink, be drunk and vomit, fall and rise no more, because of the sword which I am sending among you.' And if they refuse to accept the cup from your hand to drink, then you shall say to them, 'Thus says the LORD of hosts: You must drink! For behold, I begin to work evil at the city which is called by my name' " (Jer. 25:27–29; cf. Ezek. 23:31–35). According to Hab. 2:15–16, a nation that plunders and lays waste another nation will also drink the cup of divine wrath. The cup of wrath consists of the judgments which God has threatened and executed upon Israel, the church, and the nations. These judgments are signs of the cup of wrath which Jesus drank for all nations and for Israel and the church. In the Garden of Gethsemane he fell on his face and prayed in great agony of spirit three times: "My Father, if it be possible, let this cup pass from me; nevertheless, not as I will, but as thou wilt" (Matt. 26:36–46 and par.). There in the garden the Savior of the world gazed into a cup that made him shudder. "His sweat became like great drops of blood." (Luke 22:44.) He drank the cup that was filled to the brim with God's holy wrath against his people and the nations of the world. He tasted its bitter dregs to the very end—a cup of unspeakable horror and utter desolation. When the cup was empty, he could cry: "It is

finished." Since that hour the cup of God's wrath has become the cup of salvation and blessing, the cup of reconciliation and peace.

> Death and the curse were in our cup;
>   O Christ, 'twas full for Thee!
> But Thou hast drained the last dark drop;
>   'Tis empty now for me:
> That bitter cup,
> Love drank it up;
>   Now blessing's draught for me.
>   (Anne Ross Cousin, 1824–1906)

The cup we now drink in thanksgiving, love, and hope can only be a remembrance, a proclamation, of the cup Jesus drank for us.

16. Rudolf Bultmann thinks that by "living water" is not meant the Spirit at all but rather the revelation which is identical with the person of the revealer. (*The Gospel of John: A Commentary*, tr. by G. R. Beasley-Murray *et al.*; The Westminster Press, 1971, pp. 181 ff.) Oscar Cullmann agrees that Bultmann "is right thus far that Jesus himself is, when all is said and done, the gift itself, but on the other hand he is also the giver of the gift of the Spirit" (*Early Christian Worship*, pp. 82 f.).

17. It is an interesting fact that, though it has been claimed that there is a sacramental baptism of the Spirit in, with, and under water baptism, there is no sacrament of drinking the water of life. Perhaps it has been thought that the "sacrament" of baptism obviated the necessity for any such additional sacrament. Karl Barth has argued convincingly against water baptism being a sacrament of "the washing of regeneration and renewal in the Spirit" (Titus 3:5) in *Church Dogmatics* IV, 4. There is no need to recapitulate that material here.

Chapter 2. WHAT MEN MAY EAT AND DRINK WITH JESUS

1. Cf. Heinrich Heppe, *Reformed Dogmatics*, rev. and ed. by Ernst Bizer, tr. by G. T. Thomson (London: George Allen & Unwin, Ltd., 1950), pp. 630 f.

2. K. Barth, *Church Dogmatics* III, 4, pp. 354 f. See also *ibid.*, pp. 350–356 and III, 1, pp. 207–212.

3. H. H. Rowley has observed that in the earliest pre-Deuteronomic period "all slaughter was for sacrifice" (*Worship in Ancient Israel*, Fortress Press, 1967, p. 119). Hans-Joachim Kraus explains: "As meat was very rarely eaten in everyday life, the solemn meal which was held at a holy place . . . was marked by joy and the presence of God" (*Worship in Israel*, tr. by G. Buswell; rev. and enlarged ed. [John Knox Press, 1966], p. 118). J. Wellhausen had stated earlier that "a meal was always connected with a sacrifice. . . . Where a sacrifice took place, there was also eating and drinking. . . . There was no offering without a meal, and no meal without an offering" (*Prolegomena to the History of Ancient Israel*, tr. by J. S. Black and Allen Menzies [Meridian Books, 1957], p. 71). Later Deuteronomy provided for nonsacrificial slaughter for food (Deut. 12:15, 21 ff.), but even then only "before the LORD your God in the place which the LORD your God shall choose." Rowley is of the opinion that after its erection the Temple at Jerusalem continued to be the daily scene of private and family sacrifices (*op. cit.*, p. 119). In the later exilic and post-exilic period, when the Priestly Code seems to have been regularized, a meal no longer necessarily accompanied a sacrifice. Wellhausen, wrongly we think, saw in this development a "denaturalisation of the feasts" (*op. cit.*, p. 102). But the fact that in the "whole burnt offering" the whole of an animal or of a bird was consumed by fire on the altar "to make an atonement" (Lev., ch. 1), once in the morning and once in the evening (Ex. 29:38 ff.; Num. 28:2 ff.); that in the case of the "peace offering" the blood was thrown against the altar and the fat was burned on the altar (Lev. 3:2 ff.) and part of the flesh became the due of the priests and part was eaten by the offerer (Lev. 7:11 ff.); that in the case of the sin offering and the guilt offering the priests were permitted to eat of the flesh only after it had been offered for sin (Lev. 6:26; 7:6)—all this indicated that the flesh of animals was not intended first to be for food but belonged to God as a sacrifice and only then could be eaten.

4. K. Barth, *Church Dogmatics* III,1, p. 210.

5. In keeping with the Biblical understanding of the permission and commandment to eat the flesh of animals is the injunction to be kind to animals (Ex. 34:26; Lev. 22:28; Deut. 22:4–7;

25:4; Prov. 12:10; Luke 14:5; I Tim. 5:18; Gen. 24:19 f., 45 f.).
Cruelty to animals and birds, and shooting them merely for sport,
is reprehensible. Even the caging of them for a spectacle is highly
questionable. "Wherever man exercises his lordship over the animal, and especially across every hunting lodge, abattoir and vivi-
section chamber, there should be written in letters of fire the
words of St. Paul in Rom. 8:18 f. . . . concerning the 'earnest
expectation' . . . of the creature—for what?—for the 'manifestation of the children of God,' and therefore for the liberation of
those who now keep them imprisoned and even despatch them
from life to death. . . . A good hunter, honourable butcher and
conscientious vivisectionist will differ from the bad in the fact
that even as they are engaged in killing animals they hear this
groaning and travailing of the creature" (K. Barth, *Church Dogmatics* III,4, p. 355).

6. Gerhard von Rad, *Theologie des Alten Testaments* (Mu-
nich: Chr. Kaiser Verlag, 1966), Vol. I, p. 222. Cf. M. Noth,
The Laws in the Pentateuch, and Other Studies, tr. by D. R. Ap-
Thomas (London: Oliver & Boyd, Ltd., 1966), pp. 13, 21 ff.;
Helmer Ringgren, *Israelite Religion*, tr. by David E. Green (For-
tress Press, 1966), p. 142.

7. Calvin in his commentary (*Harmony of the Pentateuch*
[Edinburgh: Calvin Translation Society, 1853], Vol. II, p. 63)
asked how God could pronounce anything which he has created
to be unclean, since this reproach would reflect upon the Creator
and would be contrary to his declaration that everything which he
had made was "very good." Calvin's solution is that "no animal
was ever unclean in itself; it is unclean only in reference to its
use. God does not condemn his work in the animals, but, as to
their being eaten, he would have them accounted unclean, that
the people might abominate that which is forbidden them. In a
word, it is only transgression which defiles: for the animals have
never changed their nature; but it was in God's power to determine what he would have to be lawful or unlawful."

8. As long as the laws concerning clean and unclean meat remained in force, the fellowship of the church, as a fellowship of
Jews and Gentiles, was virtually impossible. They could not eat
and drink together. They could not partake of the Lord's Supper

together. This was the problem that faced the early church as recorded in Acts, chs. 10; 11; 15.

9. For a discussion of the point, see Charles Bigg, *Saint Peter and Saint Jude*, 2d ed., International Critical Commentary (Alec R. Allenson, Inc., 1956); C. E. B. Cranfield, *I & II Peter and Jude*, Torch Bible Commentaries (London: SCM Press, Ltd., 1960); A. R. C. Leaney, *The Letters of Peter and Jude*, Cambridge Bible Commentary (Cambridge University Press).

10. See I Cor. 9:25; Gal. 5:23; II Peter 1:6; Titus 1:8. Proverbs teaches that because "wine is a mocker, strong drink is a brawler, and whoever is led astray by it is not wise" (Prov. 20:1) and because those "who tarry long over wine" have woe, sorrow, strife, and complaining, therefore, "do not look at wine when it is red, when it sparkles in the cup and goes down smoothly. At the last it bites like a serpent, and stings like an adder. Your eyes will see strange things, and your mind utter perverse things" (Prov. 23:29–33; cf. vs. 20–21). The prophet Isaiah warns: "Woe to those who rise early in the morning, that they may run after strong drink, who tarry late in the evening till wine inflames them" (Isa. 5:11 f.; cf. chs. 5:22; 28:1, 7 f.). Instances of debauchery and revelry are condemned and punished, whether in the case of Noah, the preacher of righteousness (Gen. 9:20 ff.), or of Nabal, the foolish husband of Abigail (I Sam. 25:36 ff.), or of Benhadad the king of Syria (I Kings 20:12, 16), or of King Belshazzar (Dan. 5:1–4, 22–30). Proverbs counsels temperance. "If you have found honey, eat only enough for you, lest you be sated with it and vomit it." (Prov. 25:16; cf. ch. 30:7–8.)

11. The law governing the Nazirites is recorded in Num. 6:1–21 and required among other things that "he shall separate himself from wine and strong drink, and shall not drink any juice of grapes or eat grapes, fresh or dried. All the days of his separation he shall eat nothing that is produced by the grapevine, not even the seeds or skins." During the time of his separation no razor was to come upon his head. The Nazirites took a voluntary vow to devote themselves wholly to the Lord for a season. However, there were some who were lifelong Nazirites. Samson confessed to Delilah: "A razor has never come upon my head; for I have been a Nazirite to God from my mother's womb" (Judg. 16:17; cf. ch.

13:4 f., 14). Hannah, the mother of Samuel, vowed: "O LORD of hosts, if thou wilt indeed look on the affliction of thy maidservant . . . but wilt give to thy maidservant a son, then I will give him to the LORD all the days of his life, and no razor shall touch his head" (I Sam. 1:11; cf. chs. 1:28; 2:20). Elizabeth, the mother of John the Baptist, was told by the angel that her son "shall drink no wine nor strong drink" (Luke 1:15), and John's food was "locusts and wild honey" (Matt. 3:4; Mark 1:6) and he "came neither eating nor drinking" (Matt. 11:18; Luke 7:33). The prophet Jeremiah made an example of the obedience of the Rechabites to a vow they had made to their earthly father to reproach the disobedience of the Israelites to God. They had vowed "to drink no wine all our days, ourselves, our wives, our sons, or our daughters, and not to build houses to dwell in" (Jer. 35:8 f.). The reason for their obedience was that they might "live many days in the land where you sojourn"—an obvious reference to the Fifth Commandment with its promise (Ex. 20:12).

12. Cf. Gerhard von Rad, *Theologie des Alten Testaments* (Munich: Chr. Kaiser Verlag, 1966), Vol. I, pp. 76 ff.; Walter Eichrodt, *Theology of the Old Testament*, tr. by J. A. Baker, Vol. I (The Westminster Press, 1961), pp. 303 ff.; J. Pedersen, *Israel*, Vols. III–IV (London: Oxford University Press, 1940), pp. 264 ff.

13. Jesus' own disciples had left everything to follow him: houses, lands, brothers, parents, and children (Matt. 19:27, 29). Their renunciation of money and property, of personal honor and prestige (Matt. 23:5–12), of reliance upon political power (Matt. 26:52) of family (Matt. 10:37 ff.; Luke 14:25 ff.), and of self-assertion (Matt. 16:24 f.) were extraordinary signs that "the form of this world is passing away" (I Cor. 7:31) and that the follower of Jesus must not "be conformed to this world" (Rom. 12:2). The life-style of the disciples was not intended to be a general rule binding on all Christians, for elsewhere Scripture grants the freedom to marry, earn money, hold property, and to eat and drink all things.

14. The New Testament uses the words πρόσκομμα ("stumbling block") and σκάνδαλον ("offense") in two ways: first with reference to Christ (Rom. 9:32 f.; 11:9; I Cor. 1:23; I Peter 2:6 ff.), and second, with reference to differences of opinion among Christians (Rom., ch. 14; I Cor., chs. 8 and 10). The for-

mer, the offense of Christ, is unavoidable and is overcome only through faith (Rom. 9:33); the latter must be unconditionally avoided. Anything that might shake fellow Christians in their faith or might keep others from coming to faith has to be shunned. For the meaning and use of words associated with πρόσκομμα and σκάνδαλον see *Theological Dictionary of the New Testament*, Vol. VI, pp. 745–758, and Vol. VII, pp. 339–358.

15. K. Barth, *Church Dogmatics* III, 1, p. 209. Cf. Gen. 9:4–6; Lev. 3:17; 7:26 f.; 17:10–14; Deut. 12:15 f., 23–25; I Sam. 14:32–35.

16. In II Kings 6:24–33 it is related that there was a great famine in Samaria while it was besieged by the army of Syria. The price of food, even for an ass's head or a dove's dung, was so exorbitant that two women agreed to kill their sons and eat them. So they boiled one son and ate him. The next day one of the women hid her son and the other complained to the unnamed king of Israel who was passing by. When he heard the words of the woman he rent his clothes and put on sackcloth and, blaming Elisha for this fearful judgment, vowed to take off the prophet's head. Elsewhere in Scripture eating the flesh of one's kinsmen is regarded as one of the most frightful of the consequences of disobedience. "And you shall eat the offspring of your own body, the flesh of your sons and daughters, whom the LORD your God has given you, in the siege and in the distress with which your enemies shall distress you." (Deut. 28:53.) So desperate and so inhuman will even the most sensitive and compassionate become that "the man who is the most tender and delicately bred among you will grudge food to his brother, to the wife of his bosom, and to the last of the children who remain to him; so that he will not give to any of them any of the flesh of his children whom he is eating, because he has nothing left him, in the siege and in the distress with which your enemy shall distress you in all your towns. The most tender and delicately bred woman among you, who would not venture to set the sole of her foot upon the ground because she is so delicate and tender, will grudge to the husband of her bosom, to her son and to her daughter, her afterbirth that comes out from between her feet and her children whom she bears, because she will eat them secretly, for want of all things, in the siege and in the distress with which your enemy shall dis-

tress you in your towns." (Deut. 28:54–57; cf. Lev. 26:27 ff.; Isa. 9:19 ff.; Jer. 19:9; Lam. 2:20; 4:10; Ezek. 5:10.) And the same judgment is threatened against Israel's oppressors (Isa. 49:24 ff.).

17. Cannibalistic practices may be classified under two main heads: (a) food cannibalism, and (b) ritualistic cannibalism. Food cannibalism has been practiced for the satisfaction of hunger as a result of dire necessity or to gratify a taste for human flesh. It has been found among tribes in West Africa and the Indian tribes of North America, but also among civilized races, as the records of sieges and shipwrecks show. Ritualistic cannibalism, on the other hand, is the eating and drinking of human flesh and blood in order to acquire the life, virtue, and power of the victim. The eating of the heart of a lion is recommended for a warrior to make him brave. Similar motives have led to the eating of those slain in battle, both friends and foes. According to J. A. Mac-Culloch, "this sacramental transfusion of qualities and energies must have originated in early times, while it is found universally among all peoples of a low range of culture. It was also aided by the growing magical theory of things, and especially by that branch of it by which it was held that the part was equal to the whole, or could convey the qualities of the whole, since the nature of anything adheres to its parts even when they are separated from it. Hence, to eat even a small piece of the flesh of beast or man would result in the assimilation of his qualities by the eater." Religious cannibalism represents a blending of magic and animism. "The belief that by eating the dead one acquires their strength is scarcely to be distinguished from the purely animistic motive— to obtain their soul." Religious cannibalism was connected with all sorts of ceremonial and ritualistic regulations. Cf. J. A. Mac-Culloch, art. "Cannibalism," *Encyclopedia of Religion and Ethics*, ed. by James Hastings (Charles Scribner's Sons, 1928), Vol. III, pp. 197 ff.

Chapter 3. How Men May Eat and Drink with Jesus

1. Cf. S. Kierkegaard's discussion of the Socratic understanding of knowledge in *Philosophical Fragments*, tr. by Walter Lowrie, 2d ed. (Princeton University Press, 1962).

2. We have presented, with, it is hoped, some precision and

with appropriate clarifications, the usual interpretation of Jesus' command: "Do this in remembrance of me," namely, that we are to eat and drink in remembrance of Jesus and his death. However, J. Jeremias has offered the novel theory that the command may be translated, "This do, that God may remember me," that is, that God may remember the Messiah by bringing about his kingdom in the parousia (*The Eucharistic Words of Jesus*, 1966, pp. 237–255). His somewhat strained exegesis has not found acceptance among scholars. D. Jones ("ἀνάμνησις in the LXX and the Interpretation of I Corinthians 11:25," *Journal of Theological Studies*, N.S., Vol. 6 [1955], pp. 183–191), and H. Kosmala ("'Das tut zu meinem Gedächtnis,'" *Novum Testamentum*, Vol. 4 [1960], pp. 81–94) have convincingly shown that this interpretation is highly improbable. Cf. also O. Michel's review of J. Jeremias, "Die Abendmahlsworte Jesu," 2d ed., 1949, in *Verkündigung und Forschung*, 1950, pp. 224 f.; E. Schweizer, *The Lord's Supper According to the New Testament*, p. 13; Norman Hook, *The Eucharist in the New Testament*, pp. 128–131, 144–150. A. J. B. Higgins (*The Lord's Supper in the New Testament*, p. 55) states that Jeremias' interpretation has been proved untenable by W. C. van Unnik, "Kanttekeningen bij een nieuwe verklaring van de Anamnese-woorden" in *Nederlands Theologisch Tijdschrift* Vol. IV, No. 6 (Aug., 1950), pp. 369–377. Van Unnik characterizes the proclamation of the Lord's death in I Cor. 11:26 as Paul's paraphrase of "Do this in remembrance of me." Because of my ignorance of the Dutch language I have been unable to consult this article. Cf. further J. Behm, art. "ἀνάμνησις," *Theological Dictionary of the New Testament*, Vol. I, pp. 348 f.; N. A. Dahl, "Anamnesis. Mémoire et commémoration dans le christianisme primitif," *Studia Theologica*, Vol. I, Fasc. I–II (1948), pp. 69–95; Jakob J. Petuchowski, "Do This in Remembrance of Me," *Journal of Biblical Literature*, Vol. 76 (1957), pp. 293 ff.; Marjorie H. Sykes, "The Eucharist as 'Anamnesis,'" *The Expository Times*, Vol. 71, pp. 115–118.

Chief among the objections to Jeremias' interpretation are that there are no New Testament parallels to a Godward memorial of Jesus as the Messiah nor could there be now that the Messiah has come; that prayers concerning the parousia of Christ are directed not to God but to Jesus himself (I Cor. 16:22; Rev. 22:17,

20); that God has remembered his holy covenant in remembrance of his mercy in sending the Messiah to redeem his people (Luke 1:54, 68–73); that his parousia is certain, only the time uncertain; that although there are both manward and Godward memorials in the Old Testament, the Passover, which is obviously the background for I Cor. 11:24 f., was a memorial which the Israelites were to observe of how God has delivered their fathers and there is nothing in the Passover memorial corresponding to the *azkarah*, the notion that God is to be induced to remember by means of some choice sacrifice (Lev. 2:2, 9; 5:12; 24:7; Num. 5:26). When Jeremias asks: "Was Jesus afraid that his disciples would forget him?" he suggests that there was more likelihood of God forgetting Jesus than the disciples forgetting him and that the church had to remind God about Jesus. As Douglas Jones points out, this interpretation "seems to come near to transforming the church into some sort of mediator between God and his Christ, presenting to the divine memory at every Eucharist the story of his obedience and sacrifice that God may remember him and so effect his vindication at the last day." We may well ask with John Knox: "Is there oblivion or forgetfulness fallen on God the Father? Hath He forgotten the death and passion of His Son, so that He needs to be brought in memory thereof by any mortal man?" (Cited by Norman Hook, *The Eucharist in the New Testament*, pp. 130 f., from W. M. F. Scott, *Theology*, Vol. LXI, No. 400, Oct., 1953.)

3. Didache 9; Ignatius of Antioch, *Philad.* (To the Philadelphians) 4, *Smyrn.* (To the Smyrnaeans) 6; Justin Martyr, *Apol. I* (First Apology) 66.

4. Cf. K. Barth's indirect Christological interpretation of the parable in *Church Dogmatics* IV, 2, pp. 21–25.

5. We cannot refrain from noting the contrast between the observance of the Eucharist in both Roman Catholic and Protestant services and the joyfulness associated with the Passover meal, not to speak of the meals the risen Christ has with his disciples. Even the hymns sung in our services are not associated with Easter, but with morbid and mournful thoughts about death. Surely Barth's criticism of Bach's *St. Matthew Passion* is to the point. "We are not disputing the purely musical greatness of this

work. But it also purports to be an exposition of Chapters 26–27 of Matthew's Gospel. And as such it can only confuse those who hear it. In an almost unbroken minor it is a wonderful cloud-pattern of sighs and lamentations and complaints, of cries of horror and sorrow and sympathy. It is a tragic ode culminating in a conventional funeral dirge ('Rest softly'). It is neither determined nor delimited by the Easter message, and Jesus never once speaks in it as the Victor. When is the Church going to realise, and to make it clear to the thousands and thousands who may have direct knowledge of the evangelical passion-story only in this form, that what we have here is only an abstraction and not the real passion of Jesus Christ?" (K. Barth, *Church Dogmatics* IV, 2, pp. 252 f.)

6. Cf. J. F. Keating, *The Agape and the Eucharist in the Early Church* (London, 1901; New York: AMS Press, Inc., 1969); R. Lee Cole, *Love-Feasts: A History of the Christian Agape* (London: Charles H. Kelly, 1916); A. J. Maclean, art. "Agape," Hastings' *Encyclopedia of Religion and Ethics*; G. Dix, *The Shape of the Liturgy*; Bo Reicke, "Diakonie, Festfreude und Zelos in Verbindung mit der altchristlichen Agapenfeier," Uppsala Universitet, Arsschrift, 1951, 5. Maclean summarizes various theories that have been proposed concerning the relation of Agape and Eucharist. (1) One widely held view is that from the beginning the Christians celebrated the Eucharist and also a common meal to which some liturgical importance was attached, and which was called, from at least the latter part of the first century, the "Agape." At first the Agape and the Eucharist were united but by reason either of abuses or of external persecution, they were separated in the latter half of the first century or the first quarter of the second. (2) According to another view, the Agape itself did not exist until the third century. It began as a private charity supper, becoming a more public institution in the fourth century. Though the early Christians had meals in common, these did not have any connection with the Eucharist. The term "Agape" in the writings of the first two centuries was another designation for the Eucharist itself. (3) In Germany, Spitta and Jülicher advanced the view that the Agape was the original institution and that the Eucharist grew out of it. This is similar to the view advanced to-

day by O. Cullmann, following H. Lietzmann. Although the term "Agape" is not mentioned in Acts and I Corinthians, there are specific references to "Agape" in Jude 12 and II Peter 2:13. The expression to "break bread" is found in Acts 2:42, 46; 20:7, 11; 27:35. Elsewhere it—or the corresponding substantive—is used in connection with the feedings of the multitudes (Matt. 14:19; 15:36 and par.), the meal at Emmaus (Luke 24:35), and the Last Supper (Matt. 26:26 and par.; I Cor. 10:16; 11:24). Maclean concludes that to "break bread" was "used in the Apostolic age sometimes of an ordinary meal and sometimes as a technical name of the Eucharist or perhaps of the Eucharist and a meal combined." He believes that in I Cor. 11:17–34 a common meal and the Eucharist were combined.

7. K. Barth, *Church Dogmatics* IV, 2, p. 731.

8. See K. Barth, *Church Dogmatics* I, 2, pp. 362–454; III, 2, pp. 274–285; IV, 2, pp. 727–840. Cf. A. Nygren, *Agape and Eros*, tr. by A. G. Hebert (London: S.P.C.K., 1932–1939); rev. ed., tr. by Philip S. Watson (The Westminster Press, 1953); and the art. "ἀγαπάω," *Theological Dictionary of the New Testament*, Vol. I.

9. Some scholars have contended that in I Cor., ch. 11, a distinction was made between a common meal called the Agape and the Lord's Supper which followed it. In support of this view the phrase "after supper" in v. 25 is cited: "In the same way also [he took] the cup, after supper, saying, 'This cup is the new covenant in my blood. Do this, as often as you drink it, in remembrance of me.'" But if the Supper were separate from the common meal, then the words concerning the bread would also have to follow "after supper." Actually the one meal is bracketed by the sentence concerning the bread and by the sentence about the cup, and both sentences clarify the meaning of a common eating and drinking. Convincing proof that the common meal was the Supper, and the Supper was the common meal, is given in vs. 20 and 27: "When you meet as a congregation, it is impossible for you to eat the Lord's Supper. . . . Anyone who eats the bread or drinks the cup of the Lord unworthily will be guilty of desecrating the body and blood of the Lord" (NEB). Clearly one meal, and not two, is described in this chapter.

10. For the above, see K. Barth, *Church Dogmatics* IV, 1, pp. 662–668. Cf. M. Barth, "A Chapter on the Church, the Body of Christ," *Interpretation*, Vol. 12 (1958); E. Best, *One Body in Christ.* (London: S.P.C.K., 1955); C. Chavasse, *The Bride of Christ.* (London: Faber & Faber, Ltd., 1940); E. Käsemann, *Leib und Leib Christi* (Tübingen: J. C. B. Mohr, 1933); E. L. Mascall, *Christ, the Christian and the Church* (London: Longmans, Green & Company, Inc., 1946); A. Nygren, *Christ and His Church*, tr. by Alan Carlsten (The Westminster Press, 1956); Pius XII, *Mystici Corporis, Acta Apostolicae sedis*, Vol. 35 (1943), pp. 193–248; A. E. J. Rawlinson, "Corpus Christi," in *Mysterium Christi*, ed. by G. K. A. Bell and G. A. Deissmann (Longmans, Green & Company, 1930); J. A. T. Robinson, *The Body*, Studies in Biblical Theology, No. 5 (Henry Regnery Co., 1952); E. Schweizer, *The Church as the Body of Christ.* (John Knox Press, 1964); L. S. Thornton, *The Common Life in the Body of Christ.* (London: The Dacre Press, 1942); L. S. Thornton, "The Body of Christ in the New Testament," in *The Apostolic Ministry*, ed. by K. E. Kirk, 2d ed. (Morehouse-Goreham Company, Inc., 1947); T. F. Torrance, *The Royal Priesthood* (Edinburgh: Oliver & Boyd, Ltd., 1955).

11. Note the play on words: κρίμα and διακρίνων in v. 29, διακρίνομεν and ἐκρινόμεθα in v. 31, κρινόμενοι and κατακριθῶμεν in v. 32, and κρίμα in v. 34.

12. For what follows, see C. E. B. Cranfield, "Diakonia in the New Testament," and G. W. H. Lampe, "Diakonia in the Early Church," in *Service in Christ: Essays Presented to Karl Barth on His 80th Birthday*, ed. by James I. McCord and T. H. L. Parker (Wm. B. Eerdmans Publishing Company, 1967). Cf. articles on διακονέω, διακονία, διάκονος, and δοῦλος in *Theological Dictionary of the New Testament*, Vol. II. The root meaning of *diakonein* is to wait on table. This is the sense in which it is used in John 2:5, 9; 12:2; and in Acts 6:2. Thus the angels are said to have waited on or ministered to Jesus (Matt. 4:11; Mark 1:13). Peter's mother-in-law, whom Jesus cured of a fever, "rose and served him" (Matt. 8:15). Martha, distracted with much serving, complained that Mary had left her "to serve alone" (Luke 10:40). According to the parable in Luke 12:35–40, the Master will "come

and serve [wait on]" his servants, though it is the duty of slaves to "wait on" their master first before they eat and drink (Luke 17:8–10). Paul wanted the slave Onesimus to "wait on" him on Philemon's behalf during his imprisonment for the gospel. From the root meaning of waiting on table, *diakonein* and its cognates are used to refer to a service of the physical and material needs of men. Thus *diakonein* is used in Matt. 25:44 to refer to the various services rendered to the hungry and thirsty, the naked, the sick, and those in prison. In Acts 11:29; 12:25; Rom. 15:25, 31; II Cor. 8:4, 19 f.; 9:1, 12 f., it has reference to the collection for the brethren in Jerusalem. In I Peter 4:11, where *diakonein* is contrasted with *lalein* ("speak"), it doubtless refers to the relief of physical needs (cf. Heb. 6:10). There are three passages in the New Testament in which *diakonos* clearly denotes the holder of a particular office: Phil. 1:1; I Tim. 3:8, 12. In Philippians the *diakonoi* are linked with, though mentioned after, the *episkopoi*. Similarly in I Timothy the section on the *diakonoi* follows immediately that on *episkopoi*. As Cranfield observes, "in neither passage are the functions of a *diakonos* indicated." But the fact that, while aptness to teach (included in the section on *episkopoi*) is omitted from the requirements of a *diakonos*, and the fact that the *diakonoi* are admonished to be "not double-tongued, not given to much wine, not greedy of filthy lucre," suggests that they held the dual office of attending tables in the church and of handling money for the assistance of the poor.

13. Justin, *Apol. I*, 65, 67.

14. Ignatius, *Trall.* (To the Trallians) 2.

15. Hippolytus, Apostolic Tradition 23.

16. There is no doubt that from an early date only the baptized were permitted to participate at the Lord's Supper. We would contend that only those who have been baptized (and confirmed, if they were baptized in infancy) should be permitted to preach, teach, pray, preside at the Supper, serve as waiters or deacons to prepare and serve the meals, and to exercise oversight in the congregation. But if the Lord's Supper is an act of love in remembrance of Jesus and in obedience to his command to feed the least of his brethren, how can it refuse food and drink to hungry unbaptized children? How can it refuse to offer hospitality to strang-

ers, if it does not refuse to them the Word of eternal life in the gospel? When a stranger is moved by the Spirit to confess Christ, he should be baptized as soon as possible and be made a "full communicant." As Geoffrey Wainwright remarks: "How long did the Philippian jailer have to wait before he was baptized . . . and the (eucharistic) table was spread (Acts 16:25–34)?" Cf. his somewhat different but careful examination of the question of the relation of Baptism to the Eucharist in *Eucharist and Eschatology*, pp. 128–135, 204. Since we have touched here upon church discipline, it is well to note that while Paul urged the Corinthians to excommunicate idolaters and immoral persons from their membership, it was to be an evangelical bann. They were to deliver the man who was living with his father's wife "to Satan for the destruction of the flesh that his spirit may be saved in the day of the Lord Jesus." The purpose of church discipline is the salvation of offenders. It is not to be exercised self-righteously or lovelessly. "Ought you not rather to mourn?"

17. While I have found extremely suggestive an offprint of a sermon by Helmut Gollwitzer on Matt. 25:31–34 for *Worte am Sonntag—heute gesagt*, Band I, 3 (Gütersloher Verlagshaus, 1973), he goes too far when he directly identifies God with the poor. It is better to keep to his own statement: " 'Gott in Christus,' wie wir theologisch sagen, das ist Gott in seinen geringsten Brüdern." Cf. Karl Barth, *Church Dogmatics* IV, 1, p. 106: "According to Mt. 25:31 f. the criterion at His judgment will be the question what we have done or not done to Him in the person of the least of His brethren. They are not identical with Him, but they are witnesses . . . of the poverty which He accepted to establish that fellowship between God and man which is given to the world and gives light to the Christian community, witnesses of the wealth which in Him is given secretly to the world and openly to the Christian community in that fellowship." Cf. also Vol. III, 2, pp. 507 f.

18. In his pioneering work *Eucharist and Eschatology*, Geoffrey Wainwright has rightly pointed out that older treatises on the Eucharist in the West dealt with the Eucharist under three aspects. First, "they dealt with the *presence* of Christ in or at the sacrament, and particularly with the relation between the bread

and the wine and that presence. . . . The notion of an *advent* of
the Lord to his people in a visitation of judgment and salvation
fared rather badly." Secondly, they were concerned with the relation between the cross of Christ and the *sacrificial* nature of the
Eucharist. "Theologians saw the Eucharist as looking back to the
past event of the Lord's death much more than as looking forward
to the *future* event of His coming; they were concerned with the
relation between present and past rather than with the relation
between present and future." Thirdly, they were concerned with
the individual communicant's present union with his Lord rather
than with the Eucharist as the common meal of the whole
churchly people of God in the last days, and with its relation to
the Messiah's banquet in the kingdom. Although eschatology has
been in vogue in the twentieth century, due to the work of New
Testament scholars, notably, Johannes Weiss, Albert Schweitzer,
C. H. Dodd, J. Jeremias, R. Bultmann, O. Cullmann, and W. G.
Kümmel, and of systematic theologians such as W. Kreck, J. Moltmann, and G. Sauter, Wainwright observes that there has not
been "anything like a satisfactory attempt to bring into systematic
relation this newly discovered eschatology and the theology of the
Eucharist."

Exegetes who have taken the eschatological dimension into
consideration in their treatments of the Lord's Supper, notably
O. Cullmann, E. Schweizer, and A. J. B. Higgins, have "worked
under the spell (whether succumbed to or struggled against) of
H. Lietzmann's theory of the two types of primitive Eucharist:
the eschatological joy-meal of the Jerusalem Church, and the
Pauline memorial of the death of Christ. They have not made too
close reference in this connection to the vexed questions of the
general eschatology of the New Testament, let alone to the systematic problems of interpreting 'present' and 'future.'" The
eschatology that informs Wainwright's own presentation is not one-
sided or extreme. It is not the futurist eschatology of A. Schweitzer, nor the realized eschatology of C. H. Dodd, nor the existen-
tialist eschatology of R. Bultmann. While critical of O. Cullmann's linear view of time, Wainwright believes that eschatology
needs the horizontal model of the *Heilsgeschichte* view and the
vertical model. He is sympathetic to W. Kreck's emphasis upon

Jesus Christ as the One who has come, who continues to come in a hidden manner, and who will come again in glory. But with J. Moltmann he wants to guard against reducing what is still to come to a "mere revelation." It is strange that Wainwright makes no mention of K. Barth's eschatology. (See *Church Dogmatics* III, 2, pp. 437–640; IV, 3, pp. 292–367, 902–942.)

The weakness of Wainwright's otherwise excellent work lies, we believe, in the acceptance of a sacramental interpretation of the Lord's Supper. He grants that "the strongest strand in biblical and dominical teaching on the relation between the eucharist and the final messianic feasting" is the view that "the eucharist is rightly, and *adequately* set into relation with the final kingdom if it is viewed as an (anticipatory) feeding *with* Christ, at His table, on the fruits of the new creation" (Wainwright's italics). But he believes that this "strongest strand . . . does not seem to do justice to the theme of John 6 and its imagery of *feeding on Christ*" (p. 106), though he adds that "it must be admitted that John 6 is the only part of the New Testament to speak directly of feeding *on* Christ." While he wishes to avoid "any doctrine of the eucharistic *elements* of bread and wine which threatens to give more prominence to Christ as food than to Christ as host and table-fellow" (p. 108), he goes on "to define more precisely a *causal relation* between eucharistic communion and participation in the kingdom of God" on the basis of his interpretation of John 6:53–58. "The sacramental food of the eucharist is our food for eternal life" (p. 111). If it does not exactly possess medicinal and remedial powers, it begins "the transformation of the communicant which . . . will be completed only through the resurrection" (pp. 112 f.). The Eucharist is not only "expressive" but "creative of the church's unity" (pp. 115–117, 141–143). But Wainwright is so cautious and reserved concerning the alleged "effects" caused by eating and drinking Christ's flesh and blood in the Eucharist that one has the impression that he does not find this train of thought too congenial to his eschatological view of the Lord's Supper. He accepts "the image of the *body of Christ* . . . as a valuable expression of the truth that it is only as we are in Christ and Christ lives in us that we share in eternal life . . . but the image is a dangerous one if it is not balanced by others"

(p. 114). Toward the end of his book Wainwright offers a number of reasons why an eschatological understanding of the Eucharist declined in the church. First, he mentions the disappointment of the church's expectation of an early parousia. He believes that this factor no longer applies to the same extent because now it is better realized that the nearness of the parousia is much more a question of quality than of chronological quantity.

But does this get at the heart of the matter? It is true that very early the church lost the New Testament's vivid sense of the imminent return of the Lord. But what evidence is there that the church was disappointed? Did it not come to understand itself as having been founded, authorized, and empowered by Jesus to be the channel and the means by which Christ and his benefits or merits were made present in and by the sacraments? Did it not believe that by means of a dramatic liturgy the events of Christ's life, including his death and resurrection, were reenacted, represented, and realized? Was not eschatology realized in the church's sacramental ministry through lawfully ordained clergy who stood in a *historical* episcopal or presbyterial succession? Could the church not then be reconciled to a belief—utterly foreign to the New Testament—in the *Parousieverzögerung* (delay of the parousia)? Indeed, have not modern Protestant scholars been repeating *ad nauseam* that Jesus, the apostles, and the early church were mistaken, deceived, deluded, and disappointed concerning the imminent return of the Lord? Have they not been perpetuating the error of the scoffers in the New Testament itself, who asked: "Where is the promise of his coming? For ever since the fathers fell asleep, all things have continued as they were from the beginning of creation" (II Peter 3:4)? Must we not take seriously Peter's admonition: "But do not ignore this one fact, beloved, that with the Lord one day is as a thousand years, and a thousand years as one day. The Lord is not slow about his promise as some count slowness, but is forbearing toward you, not wishing that any should perish, but that all should reach repentance" (II Peter 3:8 f.). If according to Rom. 15:13 we abound in hope by the power of the Holy Spirit (cf. Gal. 5:5; II Thess. 2:16), will not the Eucharist become an eschatological meal through a little experience of the consolation of the Holy Spirit himself?

19. K. Barth, *Church Dogmatics* IV, 3, p. 293. Cf. A. Oepke, art. "παρουσία," *Theological Dictionary of the New Testament,* Vol. V, pp. 858–871.

20. For the concept of the covenant, see the articles by Gottfried Quell and Johannes Behm on διαθήκη in *Theological Dictionary of the New Testament,* Vol. II, pp. 106–134; and K. Barth, *Church Dogmatics* IV, 1, pp. 22–34, 54–66.

21. Cf. G. Wainwright, *op. cit.,* pp. 19 ff.

22. "[The Church] has certainly not succeeded in making it [Israel] jealous, in making clear to it the nearness of the kingdom of the Son of David, in making Jesus of Nazareth dear and desirable and inviting to it. In this sense the Church as a whole has made no convincing impression on the Jew as a whole. It has debated with him, tolerated him, persecuted him, or abandoned him to persecution without protest. What is worse, it has made baptism an entrance card into the best European society. It has seriously sought the conversion of individuals. But for the most part it has not done for the Jews the only real thing which it can do, attesting the manifested King of Israel and Savior of the world, the imminent kingdom, in the form of the convincing witness of its own existence. And thus it still owes everything to those to whom it is indebted for everything. This failure, which is often unconscious, or perhaps concealed by all kinds of justifiable or unjustifiable countercharges against the Jews, is one of the darkest chapters in the whole history of Christianity and one of the most serious of all wounds in the body of Christ." (K. Barth, *Church Dogmatics* IV, 3, p. 878.)

23. From the hymn "Arm of the Lord, Awake, Awake!" by William Shrubsole, 1759–1829.

24. From the hymn "Zion's King Shall Reign Victorious," by Thomas Kelly, 1769–1854.

25. Cf. K. Barth, *Church Dogmatics* IV, 3, pp. 350 ff.

26. For this insight I am indebted to Walter Lüthi, "Land der Morgen," in *Was die Welt zusammenhält* (Basel: Verlag Friedrich Reinhardt A.G.).

27. The interpretations of ἐπιούσιον, found only in Matt. 6:11 and Luke 11:3, have been numerous: daily, for today, for the morrow, for the future, sufficient, necessary for existence, allotted,

appointed. John Lowe has stated: "The unpalatable fact is that we do not know the Aramaic word which lies behind ἐπιούσιος, nor the meaning of ἐπιούσιος itself, and we can only indulge in guesswork" (*The Interpretation of the Lord's Prayer* [Evanston, Ill., 1956], p. 19). Following an examination of the Codices Sergii, D. Y. Hadidian has come to the conclusion that the meaning of the verse is: "Set before us this day (or each day) the bread of continuity" ("The Meaning of ἐπιούσιος and the Codices Sergii," *New Testament Studies*, Vol. 5, 1958–1959, pp. 75–81). In recent years a number of scholars have taken the fourth petition to refer to the coming kingdom and its feast, notably, A. Schweitzer (*Die Mystik des Apostels Paulus*, 1930, pp. 233–35), J. Jeremias (*Jesus als Weltvollender*, 1930, pp. 52 f.; "Das Vater-Unser im Lichte der neueren Forschung," *Abba*, 1966, pp. 165–167), and E. Lohmeyer (*Das Vater-Unser*, 1947, pp. 92–110). G. Wainwright, after an exhaustive survey of the literature, stresses this eschatological interpretation. However, he seems to agree with Lohmeyer that "the bread for which we pray is *at one and the same time* both earthly bread to meet the hunger and need of the present day, and also the future bread which will satisfy the elect in the eschatological kingdom and is already given to us in anticipation. . . . Lohmeyer is prepared to see the church's eucharist, itself likewise standing astride present and future, as 'germinally present' in the ambivalent petition for bread in Jesus' prayer" (*op. cit.*, p. 34). Cf. Raymond E. Brown, "The Pater Noster as an Eschatological Prayer," *New Testament Essays* (Bruce Publishing Company, 1965, pp. 217–253).

28. The eating and drinking described in Rev., chs. 21 and 22, is not called the marriage supper, though the invitation to the supper is repeated in 22:17. Mathias Rissi, *The Future of the World: An Exegetical Study of Revelation 19:11–22:15* (London: SCM Press, Ltd., 1972), observes that "present day interpretation of the Revelation of John is on the whole in agreement that Rev. 19:11–16 describes the return of Christ." If this interpretation is correct, then Rev. 19:6–9 speaks of the marriage supper of the Lamb as an anticipation of his return and of an eating of the tree of life and of a drinking of the river of life in a new heaven and earth.

Appendix I. Whether Jesus Is Eaten in the Lord's Supper

1. O. Cullmann and F. J. Leenhardt, *Essays on the Lord's Supper*, tr. by J. G. Davies (John Knox Press, 1958).

2. H. Lietzmann, *Messe und Herrenmahl*, 3d ed. (Berlin, 1955).

3. *Bishop Sarapion's Prayer-Book*, ed. by John Wordsworth (Archon Books, 1964).

4. The Library of Christian Classics, Vol. I, *Early Christian Fathers*, ed. by Cyril C. Richardson *et al.* (The Westminster Press, 1953), pp. 161–179.

5. *The Treatise on the Apostolic Tradition of St. Hippolytus of Rome, Bishop and Martyr*, ed. by Gregory Dix (London: S.P.C.K., 1968).

6. Ignatius, *Eph.* (To the Ephesians) 20.

7. *Ibid.*, 5.

8. Ignatius, *Philad.* 4.

9. Ignatius, *Smyrn.* 7.

10. Ignatius, *Trall.* 2.

11. Justin, *Apol. I*, 65–67. The Library of Christian Classics, Vol. I, pp. 285–288.

12. J. H. Srawley, "Eucharist," Hasting's *Encyclopedia of Religion and Ethics*, Vol. V, p. 547.

13. Augustine, *de Cat. Rud.* XXVI.

14. Augustine, *Tract. in Johann.* XXVI, 15, 11.

15. *Ibid.*, LXXX, 3.

16. Augustine, *En. in Ps.* III, 1.

17. Augustine, *Serm.* CXII, 5.

18. Augustine, *Tract. in Johann.* XXV, 12.

19. Augustine, *En. in Ps.* I, 10.

20. *Ibid.*, II, 2.

21. Augustine, *Serm.* CCXXXIV, 2.

22. Darwell Stone, A *History of the Doctrine of the Holy Eucharist*, Vol. I (1909), p. 83.

23. Augustine, *On Baptism*, V, 9.

24. Augustine, *Serm.* LXXI, 17.

25. We shall forgo a discussion of the development of the

conception of the Eucharist as a sacrifice and of the development of Ignatius' idea that it is "the medicine of immortality." Nor will we show how the rise of sacerdotalism was a natural and inevitable outgrowth of sacramentalism. To this day the one essential difference between the so-called clergy and the laity has been the power of the former to administer the sacraments. Nor will we discuss the tortuous debates in the sixteenth century which unhappily led to the schism between the Lutherans and the Reformed. For a comprehensive history, see Darwell Stone, *A History of the Doctrine of the Holy Eucharist*, Vols. I and II, 1909.

26. See appended bibliography for a list of Zwingli's works on the sacraments.

27. Zwingli, *Latin Works*, Vol. III, p. 181.

28. *Ibid.*, p. 181.

29. *Ibid.*, p. 182.

30. *Ibid.*, p. 182.

31. *Ibid.*, p. 183.

32. *Ibid.*, p. 184.

33. The Library of Christian Classics, Vol. XXIV, p. 131.

34. Zwingli, *Latin Works*, Vol. II, p. 46.

35. *Ibid.*, pp. 47 f.

36. A translation of Eck's "Refutation" is to be found in Zwingli, *Latin Works*, Vol. II.

37. *Ibid.*, p. 112.

38. *Ibid.*, p. 113.

39. *Ibid.*, p. 117.

40. *Ibid.*, p. 117.

41. *Ibid.*, p. 122.

42. *Ibid.*, p. 124.

43. *Ibid.*, p. 124.

44. The Library of Christian Classics, Vol. XXIV, p. 258.

45. *Ibid.*, p. 258.

46. At the conclusion of his treatment of the omnipresence of God in *Church Dogmatics* (II, 1, p. 487), Karl Barth referred to "the unfortunate controversy which arose out of the eucharistic conflict and in the 16th and 17th centuries separated the Lutheran and Reformed Schools in respect of the ubiquity of the human nature of Christ and especially the ubiquity of His body."

Barth showed how both sides went astray through an erroneous understanding of Christ's omnipresence and proposed a new statement which he hoped would overcome the distressing schism in the evangelical church.

47. K. Barth, *Church Dogmatics* IV, 4, p. 128.

48. Richard Reitzenstein, *Die hellenistischen Mysterienreligionen,* 3d ed. (Stuttgart, 1927); *Das iranische Erlösungs-mysterium* (Leipzig, 1921); *Die Vorgeschichte der christlichen Taufe* (Berlin, 1929).

49. The fifth and sixth editions appeared in 1964 and 1967 with a foreword by R. Bultmann.

50. Hugo Rahner, *Greek Myths and Christian Mystery* (Harper & Row, Publishers, Inc., 1963), p. 8.

51. *Ibid.,* p. 9.

52. F. Cumont, *The Oriental Religions in Roman Paganism,* tr. by Grant Showerman (Open Court Publishing Co., 1911).

53. C. Clemen, *Religionsgeschichtliche Erklärung des Neuen Testament* (Giessen: Töpelmann, 1909); *Der Einfluss der Mysterienreligionen auf das älteste Christentum* (Giessen: Töpelmann, 1913).

54. Rahner, *op. cit.,* p. 10.

55. *Evangelisches Kirchenlexikon,* Vol. II (Göttingen, 1958), p. 1475.

56. *Theological Dictionary of the New Testament,* Vol. IV, p. 824.

57. K. Barth, *Church Dogmatics* IV, 4, pp. 109 f.

58. Cf. A. J. B. Higgins, *The Lord's Supper in the New Testament,* pp. 20 f.; J. Jeremias, *The Eucharistic Words of Jesus,* pp. 84 ff.

59. E. Schweizer, *The Lord's Supper According to the New Testament,* p. 31.

60. R. Fuller, *The Mission and Achievement of Jesus,* pp. 70–71.

61. "Sacrament and the Common Meal," *Studies in the Gospels: Essays in Memory of R. H. Lightfoot,* ed. by D. E. Nineham (Oxford: B. Blackwell, 1955), p. 203.

62. Jeremias, *op. cit.,* pp. 211 f.

63. Higgins, *op. cit.,* pp. 52 f.

64. The longer form is found in the earliest uncials, Sinaiticus, Alexandrinus, Vaticanus, Ephraemi, Freerianus (Aleph, ABCW), and in the vast majority of the later MSS. and versions. The shorter form is found in the Codex Bezae (D), in several MSS. of the Old Latin version, and in the Syriac versions. For an extensive discussion of the long and the short texts, see J. Jeremias, *op. cit.*, pp. 128–159; *The Ministry and the Sacraments*, ed. by R. Dunkerley, pp. 274–286.

65. For the exegesis of John 6:51–58, cf. the following: C. K. Barrett, *The Gospel According to St. John* (London: S.P.C.K., 1962), and *New Testament Essays* (London: S.P.C.K., 1972); J. H. Bernard, *The Gospel According to St. John*, International Critical Commentary, Vol. I. (Charles Scribner's Sons, 1929); P. Borgen, *Bread from Heaven* (Leiden: E. J. Brill, 1965); G. Bornkamm, "Die eucharistische Rede im Johannes-Evangelium," *Zeitschrift für die neutestamentliche Wissenschaft*, Vol. 47 (1956); O. S. Brooks, "Johannine Eucharist: Another Interpretation," *Journal of Biblical Literature*, Vol. 82 (1963); Raymond E. Brown, *The Gospel According to John*; J. Edgar Bruns, *The Art and Thought of John* (Herder & Herder, Inc., 1969); R. Bultmann, *The Gospel of John*; John Calvin, *The Gospel According to St. John, 1–10*, Calvin's Commentaries, ed. by D. W. and T. F. Torrance (Wm. B. Eerdmans Publishing Co., 1959); C. H. Dodd, *The Interpretation of the Fourth Gospel* (Cambridge University Press, 1953); James D. G. Dunn, "John VI—A Eucharistic Discourse?" *New Testament Studies*, Vol. 17 (1970); E. C. Hoskyns, *The Fourth Gospel*; A. M. Hunter, *The Gospel According to John* (Cambridge University Press, 1965); E. Lohse, "Wort und Sakrament im Johannesevangelium," *New Testament Studies*, Vol. 7 (1960–1961); Martin Luther, *Sermons on the Gospel of St. John: Chs. 6–8*, Luther's Works, Vol. XXIII (Concordia Publishing House, 1959); G. H. C. MacGregor, "Eucharist in the Fourth Gospel," *New Testament Studies*, Vol. 9 (1963); John Marsh, *The Gospel of St. John* (Penguin Books, Ltd., 1968); Francis John Moore, "Eating the Flesh and Drinking the Blood: A Reconsideration," *Anglican Theological Review*, Vol. 48 (1966); Leon Morris, *The Gospel According to John* (Wm. B. Eerdmans Publishing Co., 1971); V. Ruland, "Sign and Sacrament; John's Bread of Life Discourse (Chap. 6)," *Interpretation*, Vol. 18

(1964); J. N. Sanders and B. A. Mastin, *A Commentary on the Gospel According to St. John* (Harper & Row, Publishers, Inc., 1968); H. Schürmann, "Joh. vi. 51c—ein Schlüssel zur grossen johanneischen Brotrede," *Biblische Zeitschrift,* 2 (1958); W. Wilkens, "Das Abendmahlszeugnis im vierten Evangelium," *Evangelische Theologie,* Vol. 18 (1958); E. Schweizer, "Das johanneische Zeugnis vom Herrenmahl," *Evangelische Theologie,* Vol. 12 (1952–1953).

66. Brown, *The Gospel According to John,* p. 274.

67. Bultmann, *The Gospel of John,* pp. 234–237. But see the article by James D. G. Dunn for a critique of Bultmann's thesis.

68. A remarkable parallel may be found in Jonah 1:11–15. "Then they [the sailors] said to Jonah, 'What shall we do to you, that the sea may quiet down for us?' For the sea grew more and more tempestuous. He said to them, 'Take me up and throw me into the sea; then the sea will quiet down for you; for I know it is because of me that this great tempest has come upon you.' Nevertheless the men rowed hard to bring the ship back to land, but they could not, for the sea grew more and more tempestuous against them. Therefore they cried to the Lord, 'We beseech thee, O Lord, let us not perish for this man's life, and lay not on us innocent blood; for thou, O Lord, hast done as it pleased thee.' So they took up Jonah and threw him into the sea; and the sea ceased from its raging." Thus were the Gentile sailors saved through the vicarious sacrifice of Jonah and through their shedding of innocent blood—a sign of "one greater than Jonah."

69. Of course the New Testament knows of another abiding or dwelling of Christ in believers through the Holy Spirit (cf. John 14:16 f.; 15:1–7, 10; I John 2:10, 14, 17, 24, 27, 28; 3:6, 24; 4:12–16; II John 9b), whereby there is an abiding in Christ, in his love, in his commandments, and in his doctrine. "I live, yet not I, but Christ lives in me." (Gal. 2:20, KJV.) He dwells in the hearts of men by faith (Eph. 3:17) and the Spirit dwells in them (James 4:5; Rom. 8:9, 11; I Cor. 3:16; II Cor. 6:16; II Tim. 1:14). By this second abiding through the Spirit we know that Christ is in the Father, and we in him, and he in us. But even this abiding through the Spirit is nowhere said to be the result or effect of a eucharistic eating and drinking.

Appendix II. The Case of "The Ugly, Broad Ditch"
and the Leuenberg Agreement of 1973

1. "On the Proof of the Spirit and of Power," in G. E. Lessing, *Theological Writings*, tr. by Henry Chadwick (London, 1956), p. 55.

2. K. Barth, *Church Dogmatics* IV, 1, p. 287.

3. Lessing, *op. cit.*, p. 53.

4. Søren Kierkegaard, *Concluding Unscientific Postscript*, tr. by David F. Swenson and Walter Lowrie (Princeton University Press, 1941), pp. 59–113.

5. K. Barth, *Church Dogmatics* IV, 1, pp. 283–357.

6. G. Thomasius, *Christi Person und Werk* (1888), Vol. III, 2.

7. K. Barth, *Church Dogmatics* IV, I, pp. 295 f.

8. *Ibid.*, IV, 2, p. 40; cf. pp. 50, 55, 107.

Bibliography

This list includes only those items which have to do, in whole or in part, with the Lord's Supper and with sacraments in general. Additional books, commentaries, and articles consulted are given in the Notes and References section.

Aalen, L., "Der Kampf um das Evangelium im Abendmahl," *Theologische Literaturzeitung*, Vol. 91 (1966).

Aalen, Sverre, "Das Abendmahl als Opfermahl im Neuen Testament," *Novum Testamentum*, Vol. 6 (1960).

Aulén, Gustav, *Eucharist and Sacrifice*. Tr. by Eric H. Wahlstrom. Muhlenberg Press, 1956.

Baillie, Donald M., *The Theology of the Sacraments and Other Papers*. With a biographical essay by John Baillie. Charles Scribner's Sons, 1957.

———, and Marsh, J., *Intercommunion: The Report of the Theological Commission appointed by the Continuation Committee of the World Conference on Faith and Order*. London, 1952.

Barclay, William, *The Lord's Supper*. Abingdon Press, 1967.

Barth, Karl, *Church Dogmatics*. Charles Scribner's Sons, 1936–1962. I, 1, pp. 61–79; I, 2, pp. 228–232; II, 1, pp. 487–490; IV, 1, pp. 295 f., 695 f.; IV, 2, pp. 40, 50, 54 f., 107; IV, 4 (A *Fragment: Baptism as the Foundation of the Christian Life*).

———, *The Knowledge of God and the Service of God*. London: Hodder & Stoughton, Ltd., 1938, pp. 190–216.

———, *The Teaching of the Church Regarding Baptism*. London: SCM Press, Ltd., 1948.

Barth, Markus, *Das Abendmahl: Passamahl, Bundesmahl und Messiasmahl* (*Theologische Studien*, No. 18, 1945).

————, *Die Taufe—Ein Sakrament?* Zollikon-Zurich: Evangelischer Verlag A.G., 1951.

Behm, J., art. "ἀνάμνησις," in *Theological Dictionary of the New Testament.* Ed. by Gerhard Kittel. Tr. by G. W. Bromiley. Vol. I. Wm. B. Eerdmans Publishing Company, 1964.

Berkouwer, G. C., *The Sacraments.* Tr. by Hugo Bekker. Wm. B. Eerdmans Publishing Company, 1969.

Betz, Johannes, *Die Eucharistie in der Zeit der griechischen Väter.* Vienna: Verlag Herder, 1961.

Bieder, W., "Christ the Sacrament for the World," *Theologische Zeitschrift,* Vol. 19 (1963).

Bizer, E., and Kreck, W., "Die Abendmahlslehre in den reformatorischen Bekenntnisschriften," *Theologische Existenz heute,* N.F., No. 47 (1955).

Bläser, P., "Eucharistie und Einheit der Kirche in der Verkündigung des Neuen Testaments," *Theologie und Glaube,* Vol. 50 (1960).

Boobyer, G. H., "The Eucharistic Interpretation of the Loaves in St. Mark's Gospel," *Journal of Theological Studies,* N.S., Vol. 3 (1952).

Bornkamm, G., "Herrenmahl und Kirche bei Paulus," *New Testament Studies,* Vol. 2 (1955–1956).

Bouyer, Louis, *Eucharistie: théologie et spiritualité de la prière eucharistique.* Paris: Desclée de Brouwer, 1966. E.T., C. U. Quinn, *Eucharist: Theology and Spirituality of the Eucharistic Prayer.* University of Notre Dame Press, 1968.

Bowmer, J. C., *The Lord's Supper in Methodism, 1791–1960.* London: The Epworth Press, 1961.

Brilioth, Yngve, *Eucharistic Faith and Practice, Evangelical and Catholic.* London: S.P.C.K., 1953.

Bruce, Robert, *The Mystery of the Lord's Supper.* Tr. and ed. by T. F. Torrance. London: James Clarke & Company, Ltd., 1958.

Buchrucker, Armin-Ernst, "Die Repräsentation des Opfers Christi im Abendmahl in der gegenwärtigen katholischen Theologie," *Kerygma und Dogma,* Vol. 13 (1967).

Calvin, John, *Institutes of the Christian Religion.* Ed. by John T. McNeill. Tr. by Ford Lewis Battles. The Library of Christian Classics, Vol. XX, Bk. IV, Chs. XIV to XVII. The Westminster Press, 1960.

————, *Tracts and Treatises on the Doctrine and Worship of the Church*, Vol. II. Tr. by Henry Beveridge. Calvin Translation Society, 1849. Reprint, with introduction by T. F. Torrance, Wm. B. Eerdmans Publishing Company, 1958.

Clark, F., *Eucharistic Sacrifice and the Reformation*. Paulist/Newman Press, 1960.

Clarke, N., *An Approach to the Theology of the Sacraments*. London: SCM Press, Ltd., 1956.

Cole, R. Lee, *Love-Feasts: A History of the Christian Agape*. London: Charles H. Kelley, 1916.

Cullmann, Oscar, *Early Christian Worship*. Tr. by A. S. Todd and J. B. Torrance. London: SCM Press, Ltd., 1953.

————, and Leenhardt, F. J., *Essays on the Lord's Supper*. Tr. by J. G. Davies. John Knox Press, 1958.

Dahl, N. A., "Anamnesis. Mémoire et commémoration dans le christianisme primitif," *Studia Theologica*, Vol. I, Fasc. I–II (1948).

Delling, Gerhard, "Das Abendmahlsgeschehen nach Paulus," *Kerygma und Dogma*, Vol. 10 (1964).

Delorme, J., *The Eucharist in the New Testament. A Symposium*. E.T., E. M. Stewart. Helicon Press, Inc., 1964.

de Watteville, Jean, *Le Sacrifice dans les textes eucharistiques des premiers siècles*. Neuchâtel: Delachaux & Niestlé, 1966.

Dignath, Walter, "Vom Abendmahl," *Stimme der Gemeinde*, Vol. 6 (1959).

Dix, Gregory, *The Shape of the Liturgy*, 2d ed. London: Dacre Press, 1945.

Dugmore, C. W., *The Mass and the English Reformers*. London: Macmillan and Co., Ltd., 1958.

Dunkerley, R., ed., *The Ministry and the Sacraments*. London: SCM Press, Ltd., 1937.

Ehrhardt, Arnold, "Sakrament u. Leiden," *Evangelische Theologie*, Vol. 7 (1947–1948).

Elert, Werner, *Abendmahl und Kirchengemeinschaft in der alten Kirche*. Berlin, 1954. E.T., N. E. Nagel, *Eucharist and Church Fellowship in the First Four Centuries*. Concordia Publishing House, 1966.

Eller, Vernard, *In Place of Sacraments: A Study of Baptism and the Lord's Supper*. Wm. B. Eerdmans Publishing Company, 1972.

Empie, Paul C., and McCord, James I. (eds.), *Marburg Revisited: A Reexamination of Lutheran and Reformed Traditions*. Augsburg Publishing House, 1966.

Feneberg, Rupert, *Christliche Passafeier und Abendmahl*. Munich: Kösel-Verlag, 1971.

Fischer, Robert H., "Luther's Stake in the Lord's Supper Controversy," *Dialog*, Vol. 2 (1963).

Friedrich, Gerhard, "Die beiden Erzählungen von der Speisung in Mk. 6,31–44; 8,1–9," *Theologische Zeitschrift*, Vol. 20 (1964).

Frost, S. B., "Toward a Biblical Doctrine of Holy Communion," *Canadian Journal of Theology*, Vol. 7 (1961).

Fuchs, Ernst, "Die sakramentale Einheit von Wort und Tat," *Zeitschrift für Theologie und Kirche*, Vol. 68 (1971).

Fuller, R. H., *The Mission and Achievement of Jesus*. London: SCM Press, Ltd., 1956.

———, "The Double Origin of the Eucharist," *Biblical Research*, Vol. 8 (1963).

———, "Worship, Sacraments and the Unity of the Church," *Anglican Theological Review*, Vol. 52 (1970).

Gaugler, E., *Das Abendmahl im Neuen Testament*. Basel, 1943.

Gerrish, B. A., "The Lord's Supper in the Reformed Confessions," *Theology Today*, Vol. 23 (1966–1967).

Gilmore, A., "Date and Significance of the Last Supper," *Scottish Journal of Theology*, Vol. 14 (1961).

Gollwitzer, Helmut, *Coena Domini*. Munich: Chr. Kaiser Verlag, 1937.

———, "Die Kirchengemeinschaft in der Abendmahlsgemeinschaft," *Evangelische Theologie*, Vol. 14 (1954).

Grass, Hans, *Die Abendmahlslehre bei Luther und Calvin*. Gütersloh: C. Bertelsmann Verlag, 1954.

———, "Die Arnoldsheiner Thesen u. die lutherische Abendmahlslehre," *Neue Zeitschrift für systematische Theologie*, Vol. 2 (1960).

Grislis, E., "Arnoldshain Theses on the Lord's Supper in Recent Discussion," *Lutheran Quarterly*, Vol. 13 (1961).

Gustafson, Berndt, "Kierkegaard und das Abendmahl," *Kerygma und Dogma* (1957).

Haas, Albert, "Die Abendmahlsgemeinschaft in der EKD," *Theologische Existenz heute*, No. 81 (1960).

Heising, A., *Die Botschaft der Brotvermehrung*. Stuttgart: Verlag Katholisches Bibelwerk, 1966.

Higgins, A. J. B., *The Lord's Supper in the New Testament*. Henry Regnery Co., 1952.

———, "The Origins of the Eucharist," *New Testament Studies*, Vol. 1 (1954–1955).

Hoekendijk, J. C., *The Church Inside Out*. Ed. by L. A. Hoedemaker & Pieter Tijmes. Tr. by Isaac C. Rottenberg. The Westminster Press, 1966.

Hook, Norman, *The Eucharist in the New Testament*. London: The Epworth Press, 1964.

Jeremias, J., *The Eucharistic Words of Jesus*. Tr. by Norman Perrin from 3d German ed. (1960), with author's revisions to July, 1964. Charles Scribner's Sons, 1966.

———, "The Last Supper," *Journal of Theological Studies*, Vol. 50 (1949).

Jones, D., "ἀνάμνησις in the LXX and the Interpretation of I Cor. xi,25," *Journal of Theological Studies*, N.S., Vol. 6 (1955).

Jüngel, E., "Das Sakrament—was ist das?" *Evangelische Theologie*, No. 6 (1966).

Jungmann, Josef Andreas, *The Mass of the Roman Rite*. Benziger Bros., Inc., 1961.

Käsemann, E., "The Pauline Doctrine of the Lord's Supper," in *Essays on New Testament Themes*. Tr. by W. J. Montague. London: SCM Press, Ltd., 1964.

Kilmartin, Edward J., *The Eucharist in the Primitive Church*. Prentice-Hall, Inc., 1965.

Kinder, E., "Zur Sakramentslehre," *Neue Zeitschrift für systematische Theologie*, Vol. 3 (1961).

———, "Das Evangelium Gottes: Verkündigung und Sakramentshandlungen," *Theologische Literaturzeitung*, Vol. 94 (1969).

Koch, Ottfried, *Gegenwart oder Vergegenwärtigung Christi im Abendmahl*. Munich: Claudius Verlag, 1965.

Koch, Reinhold, *Erbe und Auftrag. Das Abendmahlsgespräch in der Theologie des 20. Jahrhunderts.* Munich, 1957.

Kosmala, H., " 'Das tut zu meinem Gedächtnis,' " *Novum Testamentum*, Vol. 4 (1960).

Kreck, Walter, "Die reformierten Abendmahlslehre angesichts der heutigen exegetischen Situation," *Evangelische Theologie*, Vol. 14 (1954).

Krodel, Gottfried G., "The Lord's Supper in the Theology of the Young Luther," *Lutheran Quarterly*, Vol. 13 (1961).

Küng, Hans, ed., *The Sacraments: An Ecumenical Dilemma* (Concilium, Vol. 24). The Paulist Press, 1967.

Leaney, A. R. C., "What Was the Lord's Supper?" *Theology*, Vol. 70 (1967).

Leenhardt, F. J., *Le Sacrement de la Sainte Cène*. Neuchâtel: Delachaux & Niestlé, 1948.

———, *Ceci est mon Corps. Explication de ces paroles de Jésus-Christ*. Neuchâtel: Delachaux & Niestlé, 1955.

Lehmann, Helmut T., ed., *Meaning and Practice of the Lord's Supper*. Muhlenberg Press, 1961.

Lietzmann, H., *Messe und Herrenmahl*. Berlin: Walter de Gruyter. 3d ed., 1955. E.T., Dorothea H. G. Reeve, *Mass and the Lord's Supper: A Study in the History of the Liturgy*, with introduction and supplementary essay by R. D. Richardson. Leiden: E. J. Brill, 1953.

Linke, Karl, "Das Abendmahl," *Stimme der Gemeinde*, Vol. 11 (1967).

Lohmeyer, E., *Lord of the Temple: A Study of the Relation Between Cult and Gospel*. Tr. by Stewart Todd. John Knox Press, 1961.

Luther, Martin, *Luther's Works*, Vol. 36, *Word and Sacrament*. Ed. by Abdel Ross Wentz. Muhlenberg Press, 1959.

Lüthi, Walter, and Thurneysen, Eduard, *Preaching, Confession, the Lord's Supper*. Tr. by Francis J. Brooke. John Knox Press, 1960.

McCormick, Scott, *The Lord's Supper*. The Westminster Press, 1966.

McDonnell, K., *John Calvin, the Church and the Eucharist*. Princeton University Press, 1967.

Maclean, J. A., art. "Agape," *Hasting's Encyclopedia of Religion and Ethics*, Vol. I. Charles Scribner's Sons, 1908.

Maron, Gottfried, "Maria und die Eucharistie," *Evangelische Theologie*, Vol. 22 (1962).

Martimort, Aimé Georges, *The Signs of the Covenant*. The Liturgical Press, 1963.

Marxsen, Willi, "Der Ursprung des Abendmahls," *Evangelische Theologie*, Vol. 12 (1952–1953).

————, *Das Abendmahl als christologisches Problem*. Gütersloh: Gütersloher Verlagshaus Gerd Mohn, 1963.

Mastin, B. A., "Jesus Said Grace," *Scottish Journal of Theology*, Vol. 24 (1971), No. 4.

Neuenzeit, Paul, *Das Herrenmahl*. Munich: Kösel-Verlag, 1960.

Neumann, Gerhard J., "The Anabaptist Position on Baptism and the Lord's Supper," *Mennonite Quarterly Review*, Vol. 35 (1961).

Nicolas, Maria Josephus, *What Is the Eucharist?* Twentieth Century Encyclopedia of Catholicism, Vol. 52. Hawthorn Books, Inc., 1960.

Nissiotis, N. A., "Worship, Eucharist and 'Intercommunion': An Orthodox Reflection," *Studia Liturgica*, Vol. 2 (1963).

O'Shea, William J., *Sacraments of Initiation*. Prentice-Hall, Inc., 1966.

Oulton, J. E. L., *Holy Communion and Holy Spirit*. London: S.P.C.K., 1951.

Peters, A., "Zur Kritik an den Abendmahlsthesen von Arnoldshain," *Neue Zeitschrift für systematische Theologie*, Vol. 2 (1960).

Petuchowski, Jakob J., "Do This in Remembrance of Me," *Journal of Biblical Literature*, Vol. 76 (1957).

Philippi, P., *Abendmahlsfeier und Wirklichkeit der Gemeinde*. Berlin: Evangelische Verlagsanstalt, 1960.

Powers, J. M., *Eucharistic Theology*. Herder & Herder, Inc., 1967.

Rahner, Karl, *The Church and the Sacraments*. Tr. by W. J. O'Hara. Herder & Herder, Inc., 1963.

Rattenburg, John Ernest, *The Eucharistic Hymns of John and Charles Wesley*. London: The Epworth Press, 1948.

Reicke, Bo, "Die Mahlzeit mit Paulus auf den Wellen des Mittelmeers Acts 27, 33–38," *Theologische Zeitschrift*, Vol. 4 (1948).

————, *Diakonia, Festfreude und Zelos in Verbindung mit der altchristlichen Agapenfeier.* Uppsala, 1951.

Richardson, C. C., *Zwingli and Cranmer on the Eucharist.* Seabury-Western Theological Seminary, 1949.

———, "Cranmer and the Analysis of Eucharistic Doctrine," *Journal of Theological Studies,* N.S., Vol. 16 (1965).

Rietschel, E., "Der Sinn des Abendmahls nach Paulus," *Evangelische Theologie,* Vol. 18 (1958).

Rordorf, Willy, "Le sacrifice eucharistique," *Theologische Zeitschrift,* Vol. 25 (1969).

Sanders, Paul S., "Wesley's Eucharistic Faith and Practice," *Anglican Theological Review,* Vol. 48 (1966).

Sasse, H., *This Is My Body; Luther's Contention for the Real Presence in the Sacrament of the Altar.* Augsburg Publishing House, 1959.

Schenk, Wolfgang, "Zum Gebrauch von I Kor. 11,29 in der Konfirmationsdebatte," *Evangelische Theologie,* Vol. 21 (1961).

Schillebeeckx, E., *Christ the Sacrament of the Encounter with God.* Sheed & Ward, Inc., 1963.

———, *The Eucharist.* Tr. by N. D. Smith. London: Sheed & Ward, Ltd., 1968.

Schmidt, K. L., "Abendmahl im Neuen Testament," in *Die Religion in Geschichte und Gegenwart,* 2d ed., Vol. I. Tübingen: J. C. B. Mohr, 1927.

Schweizer, Eduard, *The Lord's Supper According to the New Testament.* Tr. by James Davis from 3d ed. of *Die Religion in Geschichte und Gegenwart,* Vol. I. Fortress Press, 1967.

———, "Das Abendmahl eine Vergegenwärtigung des Todes Jesu oder ein eschatologisches Freudenmahl?" *Theologische Zeitschrift,* Vol. 2 (1946).

———, "Das johanneische Zeugnis vom Herrenmahl," *Evangelische Theologie,* Vol. 12 (1952–1953).

Skibbe, E., "Discussion of Intercommunion in German Protestantism," *Lutheran Quarterly,* Vol. 11 (1959).

———, "Reaction to the Arnoldshain Theses," *Lutheran Quarterly,* Vol. 12 (1960).

Sloyan, G. S., " 'Primitive' and 'Pauline' Concepts of the Eucharist," *Catholic Biblical Quarterly,* Vol. 23 (1961).

Srawley, J. H., "Eucharist," in *Hasting's Encyclopedia of Religion and Ethics*, Vol. V. Charles Scribner's Sons, 1912.

Steinbeck, Joh., "Das Abendmahl Jesu unter Berücksichtigung moderner Forschung," *Novum Testamentum*, Vol. 3 (1959).

Stibbs, Alan Marshall, *Sacrament, Sacrifice and Eucharist*. London: Tyndale Press, 1961.

Stone, Darwell, A *History of the Doctrine of the Holy Eucharist*, Vols. I & II. London: Longmans, Green & Co., 1909.

Sykes, M. H., "The Eucharist as 'Anamnesis,'" *The Expository Times*, Vol. 71 (1959–1960).

Thomson, Ian, An *Experiment in Worship: The Revival of the Agape*. London: SCM Press, Ltd., 1951.

Thurian, M., *The Eucharistic Memorial*. Tr. by J. G. Davies. John Knox Press, 1961.

———, *The Eucharistic Liturgy of Taizé*. Tr. by John Arnold. London: The Faith Press, 1962.

———, *The One Bread*. Tr. by Theodore DuBois. Sheed & Ward, Inc., 1969.

Van Iersel, B., "Die wunderbare Speisung u. das Abendmahl in der synoptischen Tradition," *Novum Testamentum*, Vol. 7 (1964).

Visscher, L., "Questions on the Eucharist, Its Past and Future Celebration," *Studia Liturgica*, Vol. 5 (1966).

Von Allmen, Jean-Jacques, *Essai sur le Repas du Seigneur*, Cahiers Théologiques, No. 55. Neuchâtel: Delachaux & Niestlé, 1966. E.T., W. Fletcher Fleet, *The Lord's Supper*. John Knox Press, 1969.

Wainwright, Geoffrey, *Eucharist and Eschatology*. London: The Epworth Press, 1971.

Wallace, R. S., *Calvin's Doctrine of the Word and Sacrament*. Edinburgh: Oliver & Boyd, Ltd., 1953.

Williams, R. R., ed., *Word and Sacrament*. (Papers and discussions at the second theological conference between representatives of the Church of England and of the Evangelical Church in Germany.) London: S.P.C.K., 1968. (Contains English translation of the Arnoldshain Theses from the *Ecumenical Review*, Vol. XI, Jan., 1959.)

Zwingli, Huldreich. (For the original Latin and German titles of the following complete list of Zwingli's publications on the sacraments, see *Zwingli-Bibliographie*. Ed. by Georg Finsler. Zurich, 1897. Reprint, Nieuwkoop: B. De Graaf, 1962.)

————, "The Sixty-seven Articles of 1523," in *Reformed Confessions of the 16th Century*, ed. by Arthur C. Cochrane. The Westminster Press, 1966.

————, "An Account of the Faith of Huldreich Zwingli, Submitted to the German Emperor Charles V at the Diet of Augsburg" (July 3, 1530), *Latin Works of Huldreich Zwingli*, Vol. II. Ed. by Samuel Macauley Jackson. Philadelphia, 1922.

————, "Letter of Huldreich Zwingli to the Illustrious Princes Assembled at Augsburg, Regarding the Insults of Eck" (August 27, 1530). *Ibid.*

————, "A Short and Clear Exposition of the Christian Faith" (July, 1531). *Ibid.* (Another translation is to be found in The Library of Christian Classics, Vol. XXIV. The Westminster Press, 1953.)

————, "Commentary on True and False Religion" (March, 1525), *Latin Works*, Vol. III, 1929.

————, "Reply to Emser" (August 20, 1524). *Ibid.*

————, "Of Baptism" (May 27, 1525). The Library of Christian Classics, Vol. XXIV.

————, "On the Lord's Supper" (February 23, 1526). *Ibid.*

————, "Action or Use of the Lord's Supper" (April, 1525), in Bard Thompson, *Liturgies of the Western Church*. Meridian Books, The World Publishing Company, 1961.

The remainder were translated by Henry Preble and were to have been published in subsequent volumes of the *Latin Works*, under the editorship of S. M. Jackson. The project was not completed.

————, "The Canon of the Mass, Epicheresis" (August, 1523).

————, "Huldreich Zwingli's Defense of His Pamphlet on the Canon of the Mass" (1523).

————, "A Letter of Huldreich Zwingli to Matthew Alber, Preacher at Rutlingen, on the Lord's Supper" (1524).

————, "Huldreich Zwingli to Francise Lambert and All the Brethren who are Sincere in the Faith at Strassburg" (1524).

————, "About the Exclusion from the Sacrament. Zwingli's Advice to the Council at Zurich" (1525).

———, "Subsidiary Essay or Crown of the Work on the Eucharist" (1525).

———, "Reply to a Letter of Johann Bugenhagen of Pomerania" (1525).

———, "Reply to Letter of Thebald Billicanus" (1526).

———, "Reply to Letter of Urbanus Rhegius" (1526).

———, "A Friendly Exegesis or Exposition of the Matter of the Eucharist to Martin Luther" (1527).

———, "Accounts in Latin of the Marburg Conference 1528."

———, "Questions in Regard to the Sacrament of Baptism, Put to Huldreich Zwingli by a Certain Scholar" (1530).

Index of Names

Index of Subjects

208

122 ff., 127, 135
symbolically, 122
effects (efficacy):
    "antidote against
        death," 119
    cognitive, 128, 149
    confers, conveys, dis-
        penses, mediates
        grace, 125 f.
    creates church unity,
        119, 154, 177
    frees man for new life,
        new creature, 154
    justifies, grants forgive-
        ness, 126, 154
    makes holy, 125
    "medicine of immortal-
        ity," 119, 182
    participation in fruits
        of Christ's death,
        120
Eucharist (sacramental),
    119 ff., 140 f., 144, 159,
    177
Eucharist, "two types" of,
    134, 139, 148, 176
exegetical discussion of,
    134–148
historical succession (epis-
    copal, presbyterial),
    178
history of, 119–129
institution, elements con-
    secrated, 53 f., 120 ff.,
    124, 126, 133, 143, 159
means, channels, instru-
    ments:
    of faith, 9, 54, 125,
        127 f., 134
    of Holy Spirit, 37, 126

INDEX OF SUBJECTS

    of grace, 9, 54, 80, 119,
        124 ff., 128, 134, 149
    of love of God, 80
    of union with Christ,
        119 f., 154, 176
    "medicine of immortal-
        ity," 119
mystery (mystērion, sac-
    ramentum), 57, 120,
    122, 125, 131 ff., 142,
    146
mystery religions, 121 f.,
    125, 129–133, 143, 148
presence of Christ in, 54,
    57, 93, 122, 124, 126,
    128, 154, 175
presence of Christ actu-
    alized, realized, reen-
    acted, repeated, re-pre-
    sented, 9, 63, 135, 137,
    143, 147, 149, 151,
    154, 159, 178
representation of cultic
    deity, 125, 133
sacrifice, 120, 176, 182
unworthy eating, 123
virtue, 123, 154
visible sign, 122 f.
Word added to, 123

Poverty (poor), 8, 20 f., 29,
    33, 49, 74, 83, 87, 89–96,
    100, 112, 175

Riches (rich), 91–93, 100, 112

Thirst (thirsty), 28, 31–36, 74,
    93–95, 174

Work (labor, toil), 18 ff.,
    26 f., 29 f.